FREE to be ME

CW00552953

Celebrating 21 years of Freedom Youth

By Rosa Fanti and Lori Streich

◆ Tangent Books

FREE TO BE ME
First published 2016 by Tangent Books

Tangent Books
Unit 5.16 Paintworks
Bristol BS4 3EH
0117 972 0645
www.tangentbooks.co.uk
Email: richard@tangentbooks.co.uk

ISBN 978-1-910089-36-1

Authors: Rosa Fanti and Lori Streich

Design: Joe Burt (www.wildsparkdesign.com)

OFF THE RECORD *BRISTOL*

LOTTERY FUNDED

heritage
lottery fund

OutStories Bristol - Recording the lives of
lesbian, gay, bisexual and trans
people in Bristol.

Contents

Introduction

Freedom Youth celebrated its 20th Birthday in 2015. Rosa didn't want this important milestone to pass unnoticed, so we started talking with each other and then with Off the Record and Outstories about it. This led us to approach the Heritage Lottery Fund. They generously agreed to fund an oral history project to tell Freedom's story in the words of the people who set it up, who have been or are its members, and who have worked for Freedom over the years.

We interviewed 25 people, and heard from many more past and present members who filled in surveys. They spoke or wrote about the difference that being a part of Freedom has made to their lives, and how it has supported and enabled young people to be out, and to feel comfortable with their sexuality and identity. Most of all, Freedom has always been a place where young people can just enjoy themselves as themselves – whatever their identities.

Identity is an important issue for young people, and for Freedom as a whole. Over its 21 years, the whole question of identity has changed and Freedom has changed with it. Initially, Freedom Youth defined itself as an LGB group (lesbian, gay and bisexual). By 2006, it was an LGBT group (lesbian, gay, bisexual and transgender). In 2016, it is an LGBTQ+ group, widely inclusive and including those who are queer/questioning and others. We have reflected this change throughout Free to be me. We have tried to use the right abbreviation (LGB, LGBT, LGBTQ+) in the appropriate time period as we've told Freedom's story.

What hasn't changed is Freedom's core service. It has run sessions in central Bristol every Tuesday evening (barring Christmas and similar) for 21 years. It is one of the oldest, and possibly the longest continuously running social and support group for lesbian, gay, bisexual and transgender young people in the UK.

We want to thank the Heritage Lottery Fund for enabling us to record this previously hidden history, and everyone who contributed their stories and who gave their support to this project. Without you, we could not have told this story.

Thank you to

Everyone we interviewed: Adrian Murphy, Babs McPhail, Berkeley Wilde, Frederick Williams, Geo Leonard, Hannah Greenslade, Helen Webster, Henry Poultney, Issy, Julia Nibloe, Leighton De Burca, Max Thomas, Michelle McMorrow, Mo Hand, Paul Stoodley, Rachel, Rosa Fanti, Scott Morris, Stephen Williams, Sue Allen, Thom Gray, Tianna Francombe, Victoria Chalk, Susan Moores.

And to Off the Record; Outstories Bristol; Mary Milton; Kate Spreadbury; Sally Britton.

A note about the photographs: Some of the people's faces have been blanked out in the images in order to protect their identities.

What Freedom means to me

(Current Freedom members, April 2016)

"Freedom to me means freedom – being able to be ME. More than that, it means ohana – family. A sense of community and belonging. Freedom means diversity and acceptance, it means happiness and smiles and laughter. Freedom may just seem like the place I go to every Tuesday – but it is so much more than that. Freedom has completely changed my life for the better. Freedom, to me, means love."

"Freedom is a place where I have made most of my best friends. It is like a second home and while members and leaders have changed, the warmth, safety and reassurance of the group still burns bright."

"Family. Where you can be yourself."

"Freedom to me is a hug. When everywhere else feels cold or distant you can always come home to Freedom. A non-judgemental family who when you fall will help you up, or lie down with you and Just BE!"

"Freedom has given me an opportunity to meet new people and learn new things about the LGBTQ+ community. And everyone is always so nice and there is real beauty – people being themselves and fabulous."

"I've been coming to Freedom for seven years. Having this understanding has helped me feel more validated and secure."

"To me, Freedom is exactly that – the freedom to express yourself without being judged or prejudiced against."

"An opportunity to bother with being social. Meet like-minded people, learn new things with workshops, just relax and get out of all the greyness of everyday being."

"Freedom seems really cool, everyone seems really chilled and it's not as scary as I thought it would be."

"Freedom is a place where you can be yourself and no one judges you. It is a safe place."

"Lots of glitter and amazing fun."

"Freedom is a safe place to be my true self."

"To me, Freedom is a space where I can be whoever I want to be. I don't have to pretend to be one thing or another and I don't have to "prove" my "manliness". This is so important to be as being my authentic self feels amazing."

"Freedom is where I can be myself fully, chill out with friends. And I know there is always something to do!"

"Freedom is a home I can always come back to."

"Freedom is a place I can be myself and feel safe and loved for who I am."

In the beginning

1

Freedom Youth as we know it today was created in December 1995 from two independent groups, the Bristol Young Lesbian and Bisexual Group (BYLBG) which opened in 1991 and Freedom Youth, an LGB group, which started in 1995.

As early as 1990, some research was carried out by Julia Nibloe, then a student on placement from the Youth and Community Work course at Bristol Polytechnic (now known as UWE). She interviewed young women who identified as lesbian who told her that they couldn't be out in their youth club because they were frightened of being bullied, harassed or physically assaulted. They chose either not to use a service or not to come out within the youth club. *"There was nothing really very surprising in what I found but it demonstrated that the youth service, as it stood, wasn't meeting their needs."* Julia

This research identified that many young lesbians
* have low self-esteem and a negative self-identity
* are isolated with little or no friendship network
* are at risk from harm:

BRISTOL
YOUNG LESBIAN
& BISEXUAL GROUP

NEW SERVICE

WEEKLY DIRECT *PHONE LINE*
TEL: 9412989

Bristol Young Lesbian & Bisexual Group is a separate provision for young lesbians, bisexual women and young women exploring their sexuality and is led by group workers who identify as lesbian or bisexual. It offers a safe and supportive space to young women who use its service.

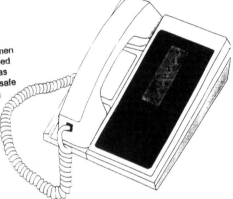

WANT MORE INFORMATION?

WHY NOT RING BRISTOL YOUNG LESBIAN AND BISEXUAL GROUPS DIRECT PHONE LINE ON WEDNESDAYS BETWEEN 12 AND 2PM AND SPEAK DIRECT TO A WORKER

- self-harm: 98% of young lesbians interviewed had either tried suicide or self-harm
- harm by others, because they are gay. All young women surveyed said they had been either physically or verbally abused because of their sexual identities.

So, a group of youth workers set about starting a Young Lesbian Group that would provide information and advice, and help to develop support and friendship networks for young women identifying as lesbian or bisexual, or who were questioning their sexuality. One of the initial aims of BYLBG was *"to provide a place where young lesbians or young women who think they might be lesbians can meet and feel accepted with ease."* Julia

A Steering Group was set up, and sessions began one evening a week in the basement room of Greenleaf Bookshop in Colston Street – a space that operated as the Bristol Women's Centre around that time. The room was offered free of charge. In time, sessions changed to Saturdays, and were run from an accessible venue in a youth centre out of the city centre. Transport was provided to enable the members to get to the sessions. Funding was also secured for a telephone helpline which ran for two hours a week.

The straightjacket of Section 28

Just setting up a group specifically for young women who were lesbian, bisexual or questioning their sexuality was a brave move. Even bolder was the decision to try to get funding from Avon County Council (the local authority that ran youth services at the time). In 1991, Section 28 was in force. This was a clause of the Local Government Act 1988 which said that

"a local authority shall not intentionally promote homosexuality, nor shall it promote the teaching in any maintained school of the

acceptability of homosexuality as a pretended family relationship."

There was no legal definition of the promotion of homosexuality, and there were never any prosecutions under Section 28. However, it created a climate of fear within local authorities and particularly in education and youth service departments and providers. BYLBG founder members aimed to work within the framework of the law, however vague the law might be. They sought advice from the County Solicitor in drafting both the aims of the group and its recruitment information – job ads and job descriptions. The solicitor's advice was that

> *"The workers will be providing support and counselling to a group of young people who have an identified need, but would not be advocating Lesbianism as a way of life, or running a dating agency, or advertising beyond the obvious required to reach affected girls. I consider that it can be argued that this is not promoting homosexuality and therefore it is not contrary to Section 28."*

Getting legal backing meant that the group also got Avon Youth Service funding. Everyone involved in setting up BYLBG and Freedom Youth said that senior officers were incredibly supportive of the need for targeted provision for young LGB people. However, there was only just enough money for BYLBG to run one session a week and occasional additional activities. And the money was never secure.

By 1994/5, the Avon Youth Service recognised and were funding BYLBG. However, there was no provision for young gay men.

> *"Nationally, the youth service was beginning to recognise that young gay men needed support. Certainly there were issues around child protection and where young men had been targeted by people who were out to sexually abuse them."* Adrian

There was also a growing concern about HIV. Although treatments were developing, the number of people diagnosed and living with HIV was still increasing. Funding was being made available to support youth work with gay men.

In 1994, Adrian Murphy, a manager in the Avon County Council Youth Service, was asked to create a project with a focus on the needs of young gay men. In January 1995, Berkeley (now Berkeley Wilde) was appointed as a gay men's health worker at Aled Richard Trust, the local organisation that focused on HIV services and support, and which merged with the Terence Higgins Trust in 2000. The idea was hatched for a group for young gay men. Conversations started and a working partnership was formed between Avon Youth Service and the Aled Richards Trust. Adrian and Berkeley started to look at widening this to include other partners including Health Promotion Service Avon (HPSA), who had funding to put into the project.

"At the time the issue of HIV was massive. The funding for the project came from HIV money in order to recognise the needs of young gay men who were facing huge issues around HIV and to create awareness of how they might protect themselves at that time." Adrian

Freedom Youth opened as a mixed, inclusive group on 4 July 1995. It was run by youth workers who were seconded by Avon Youth Service and Aled Richards Trust, and a central Bristol venue was given to the group. Freedom has used this same venue ever since. Bristol Area Health Promotion Service (BASHPS) gave a £500 grant which paid for promotion. Most of this money was used to produce the first Freedom Youth leaflet.

"On the 4th of July 1995, we opened the door. It must have been 7 o'clock and a young guy called John came through the door and we had, I think, seven young people that very first day. We'd handed out hundreds and hundreds of those rainbow leaflets at the Pride event in June that year. This was before the days of the

internet and email and social media and so everything was done by paper, put into people's hands." Berkeley

The new group was always open to young women as well as young men. With scarce resources for both BYLBG and Freedom, youth workers thought it might be an idea for both groups to work together. So, by the end of 1995, discussions started about merging Freedom Youth and BYLBG.

Freedom together

LGB youth work was a relatively small field in Bristol in the 1990s. Members of the Freedom Youth steering group knew the women who were running BYLBG who thought that there was scope for a mixed gender project. This would make the most of the energies and resources that were going into both groups. BYLBG Steering Group members could see the value in a merger. Four years after their formation, they still ran on a shoestring budget that allowed for sessional staff only, with little time for planning, preparation or follow up work. They thought that the group would be *"better together, certainly stronger"* and that a merger would create opportunities for greater resourcing of the group.

> *"It was recognised that if we worked together with Aled Richards Trust, Avon Youth Service and Health Promotion, there could be some real funding rather than just one part-time youth worker and a worker in charge which was all that was available."* Adrian

The joint group was formed "to create a healthy alliance that would offer a better service to young people and to improve management and fundraising." At a meeting on 7th February 1996, everyone agreed to name the joint organisation "Freedom". The name was approved in June 1996 after full consultation had taken place with members of both groups. It described itself as **FREEDOM: THE Lesbian and Gay Youth Organisation.**

BYLBG wound up in August 1996, and transferred £1,443.55 to the new Freedom account. The new group was established with co-chairs, one woman and one man *"so that we actually shared the responsibility between the men and the women in the group".* A great deal happened very quickly, in large measure because two key members of Freedom, Susan Moores of BYLBG and Adrian Murphy, worked well together in the Avon Youth Service.

> *"Most of it was done in our spare time, sat round tables with lots of food, in my flat or in Susan's to try and get things to work."* Adrian

Freedom ran with enthusiasm and goodwill:

> *"We didn't have any extra funding so everything was in kind: the premises, my time was given, Adrian's time was given, Bex's time was given, Susan's time was given. We only had very small pots of money to print leaflets."* Berkeley

But the first Management Group also had ambition, which prompted its members to apply to the new National Lottery for full-time funding. There was, as they all knew, a real need for Freedom.

1 FREE TO BE ME

2
Everyday homophobia

It wasn't great being gay, lesbian, bisexual or questioning in the mid 1990s. It was tough to be out, or just to be out of the norm.

MIND, the mental health organisation, had an Equalities Group that reported in 1994 that "lesbians, gay men and bisexuals do not experience mental distress or illness because of their sexuality, but the impact of heterosexism and homophobia can contribute to that distress." Eva Kosovsky Sedgewick, a leading academic in gender studies wrote in 1993 that "I think everyone who does gay and lesbian studies is haunted by the suicides of adolescents." The Bristol LGB Forum commissioned a study of lesbian, gay and bisexual Life in Bristol. Published in 1999 as Second Best Value, this found that "Homophobia remains a problem in local schools, for pupils, parents and teachers. Incidents recounted by pupils and former pupils include: 'verbal abuse', 'got bullied and accused of being a lezzie', 'general abuse/harassment', 'No sex education with positive Lesbian/Gay attitudes' and 'decided that not talking to anyone, or being friendly to anyone, was the best way to get through school… it seemed better than getting bashed.'"

And in the news....

> "Three people died and 81 were injured when a nail bomb devastated the Admiral Duncan pub in Old Compton Street, London's gay centre. The blast happened at 6.37pm without warning. The explosion shocked the gay community and ethnic minorities, coming less than a week after last Saturday's blast in Brick Lane in the East End and the previous week's nail-bomb attack on Brixton market, which injured 39." **Independent Newspaper, Friday 30 April 1999**

Venue, Bristol's fortnightly 'listings' magazine, ran a regular notice on the lesbian and gay page warning about 'queerbashing' attacks on Durdham Downs.

This was a difficult and depressing time for many LGB people.

"The 80s and 90s were just dreadful. We'd lived through the horrible Section 28 nightmare and the AIDS panic." Berkeley

"Everywhere was really homophobic then. You couldn't just walk down the street hand in hand with your partner. We were walking along Weston Pier just holding hands and got shouted abuse at, chased along the pier. Someone followed us for about ten minutes, just constantly shouting abuse at us. It was awful then. You'd go clubbing and there'd be signs in the club saying 'don't leave alone, people get beaten up, so when you leave, please leave in groups.' It's changed so much, but back then it was horrible, very homophobic." Paul

"One of our members told a teacher he was being bullied because he was gay and the teacher outed him to the rest of the group and then encouraged the others to carry on bullying him.

FACTS – about young lesbian and gay people and the impact of heterosexism and homophobia on their lives

- 6 in 10 have been verbally abused because they were lesbian or gay.
- 1 in 2 had problems at school because they were lesbian or gay.
- 1 in 5 had been beaten up because they were lesbian or gay.
- 1 in 7 had been sent to a psychiatrist because they were lesbian or gay.
- 1 in 10 had been thrown out of their home because they were lesbian or gay.
- 1 in 5 had attempted suicide because they were lesbian or gay.
- 1 in 38 said that homosexuality was mentioned in sex education at school.

From 'Something to tell you" by Lorraine Trenchard and Hugh Warren, London Gay Teenage Group (July 1984)
Quoted in Beyond a Phase, Health Promotion Service Avon (with Freedom Youth) 1998

You think 'wow' if that happened now he'd be sacked. But in '96 and '97 that behaviour was acceptable." Adrian

"We had people with placards and banners inciting hatred against gay people, and flyers you'd see on the street when you were walking back to your lift or your car after Freedom. In the back of your mind you knew that you didn't have a leg to stand on and mainstream society didn't agree with who you were and what you were. And that if push came to shove, there was nothing you could do to defend yourself. You could be in a bar or pub or club

One Last Cry for Help

We just want to live in freedom and peace
the freedom to release our inner beast.
We don't want to kill, we don't try to slay
though you say it's wrong… to be Gay
Together we fought to be equal… black or white
now yet it seems that we are without rights.
Oh why are we shunned?
Oh why are we hated?
From many a heart we are often gated.
Free will to each and every one you cry
Though if you're Gay keel over and die.
Stop all this… we are human too you see,
please leave us alone and let us be.
Oh why are we beaten? Why are we bruised?
What ever we do we seem to lose,
And now as I try to protect myself with lies
tears roll down my cheek, fallen from my eyes.
See we too have emotions
yet you continually have hate and fear locked in motion.
We just want to be free,
we just want to live,
like so many of you we have so much to give.
We are not evil,
we are not mean,
so please stop calling us… unclean.
And now it's time to restart the lies
stop the tears
and dry my eyes
and continue to hide
the precious love I hold inside.

Mark Fear, aged 15, Freedom Youth
In Beyond a Phase

or you would go to a restaurant with your friends and were told 'you're not coming because you're gay'. That happened so many times, and there was nothing you could do about it." Leighton

There is a more subtle side to the discrimination faced by LGBT young people – in the 90s and still today. Sue described a society that "puts us all into boxes" and tells us all what we are supposed to be and how to behave. Being different is difficult.

"There is a map for straight people. The structure of saying 'you go to school, you get your exams, you go to college, you go to university, you meet a wife, you settle down, you have kids'. They can choose to not be in it, but there is still a map. For LGBT people, we've got all this freedom, but we don't necessary have a map. You're born into a heterosexual environment, and that's where Freedom Youth is vital, it gives a pathway to life, it gives you a support group." Leighton

Too often in the 1990s (and even more so before) we were just invisible. For young people growing up lesbian or gay,

"There was no-one who you could look up to, no one in the public eye, on television, so you could think there are people like me out there. The only people who were portrayed as gay males were sort of overtly camp people like Larry Grayson and John Inman in 'Are You Being Served'. Maybe I'm forgetting others but that's all I can remember now. And that wasn't how I saw myself, not how the vast majority of gay men would see themselves. And certainly none in politics at that time." Stephen Williams (MP for Bristol West, 2005-2015)

And as for lesbians… what? who? where? There was TV's "first pre-watershed lesbian kiss" in 1994 on Channel 4's then popular 'Brookside'. It became one of the most talked about stories in the media at the time, and was acclaimed in about equal measure as it was reviled. But the main lesbian character, Beth Jordache, was the victim of sexual abuse from her father which led her to stab him to death and bury his body under the patio. Not exactly aspirational! In real life, there were very few out lesbians or positive role models for young women who were questioning their sexuality.

But maybe not being in the public eye had some advantages. The Huffington Post reported in 2014 that "the BBC is still receiving complaints about gay kisses on TV" in the 90s.

"There were an awful lot of negative portrayals. And even though I think I was fairly confident in my sexuality, I can't deny it was sometimes really difficult every time you'd pick up a red-top newspaper, if ever they referred to 'gay', the word pervert or paedophile or queer or poof was always referenced at the same time. That was the way things were 20 years ago." Scott

The continuing straightjacket of Section 28

Guidance issues for Bristol schools in 2003 when Section 28 was repealed states that the impact of Section 28 was out of all proportion to the narrow legal restraints which in reality it imposed. Section 28 was never directly applicable to schools but compounded by continual, erroneous reinforcement by sections of the media, many working in education were under the misapprehension that it did. They felt inhibited by what they could and could not say about sexuality. Most schools felt constrained in their abilities to tackle homophobic bullying. (Out of the Shadow: Guidance to Bristol schools on the repeal of Section 28; EACH and BCC, 2004). National research, quoted in Second Best Value, concluded that it has had a very negative impact in many schools.

On a day-to-day level, it is not clear how or how much Section 28 affected the lives of young LGB people. But we know that there

- 82% of teaches know homophobic bullying is taking place.
- Only 6% of schools have an anti-bullying policy that includes Lesbian and Gay abuse.

Report by Institute of Education, University of London 1997, Quoted in Beyond a Phase

were many, mostly unrecorded, instances of homophobia in schools that many schools were afraid of challenging. Describing the 1990s as "a dark period" for meeting the educational needs of LGB young people, Leighton talked about being unsupported.

> *"I had to move colleges twice because I was openly out. It was never an issue for my family but I went to colleges that were very conservative and they couldn't defend you from homophobia because of Section 28. The teachers couldn't step in and the institution couldn't step in."* Leighton

Or so they thought, fearing that supporting their LGB students could be interpreted as "promoting homosexuality". That wasn't what the law said or required. But in practice, *"Section 28 was a kind of carte blanche to do nothing for a lot of people."* Leighton

HIV

And as if homophobia wasn't bad enough, there was HIV. Claire Summerskill wrote, in Gateway to Heaven, that "the appearance of HIV/AIDS in the early 1980s sent shockwaves across the world, from Africa to America to Europe and back again. One of the impacts of this disease was that there was a setback in western society in the level of tolerance and understanding that gay men had been experiencing, gradually, over the previous decades." Much of the hostility was whipped up by the (mainly tabloid) press, with headlines like "AIDS is the wrath of God, says Vicar" in The Sun (February 1985) and stories about how this strange disease was "spreading like wildfire".

By the mid 1980s, the virus was dubbed the "gay plague" and stories circulated that you could catch it from using public toilets and swimming pools. AIDS "accentuated a feeling that the world was against us, and Section 28 was crucially important in confirming that." (Jeffrey Weeks, in 'Gateway to Heaven') But it has also been described as a galvanising force that politicised action on gay issues – initially around sexual health, and increasingly in a broader way. And this impacted on the development of Freedom Youth. Terence Higgins Trust, recounting the history of HIV in the 90s reports that in 1995, "the number of AIDS diagnoses in the UK reaches 10,000. More than 25,000 people in the UK are now living with HIV."

But treatments were developing: by the mid-90s combination therapies were introduced that delayed the onset of symptoms. And there was funding to deliver some work around sexual health to young gay men

> "because it was a sexual health crisis. People were dying. I was running the funerals of people at that time. So developing services for young gay men was really important and why it became a real passion to get something going." Adrian

A Freedom member from those very early days described Freedom as a real life saver.

> "If I hadn't gone to Freedom, I would probably be HIV positive now. I learned so much, it made so much of a difference."

Good to be Gay

In a world of hostility, aggression, fear and denial, Freedom became

"A safe space where young people can go and express themselves with their gender and sexual identity without a judgement call or without fear because we understand the experiences of homophobia and how devastating the consequences can be. The rage that I have about the use of homophobic language, even now, because it's so detrimental and it can affect people to the core. Those words stick. Young people have to walk around with these big coats on, carrying burdens of homophobia or transphobia that they may be experiencing. But at a place like Freedom you're not going to hear it, and so you can take your coat off." Mitch

It gave its members

"A place that you'd go that was for you, for people of your age where you could learn and meet older people who were trusted and vetted and, shall we say, not interested in 'other' things. And who helped us to deal with the day to day homophobia we faced, youth workers who were able to talk over with your situation and advise on a course of action." Leighton

Freedom was a place where it was always good to be gay.

Well, you still had to get through the door that first time… Many young people told workers that they had:

"walked around the block eight times or had arrived outside the building for three or four weeks before they felt able to come through the door. We also had a dedicated phone line in the office. So many times we would pick up the phone and there would not be any sound at the end of the line because the person was just too scared to talk. So we'd say, 'just tap the receiver so

that I know that you're still listening to me' and we would just speak about what Freedom was about." Berkeley

But

"When they walked through the door we'd say 'oh we're so pleased you're here.' At the closing round we'd ask people to say one word that describes what the next week is going to be like for you and people would say **'I'm going to be gay for the next week', because it felt good to be gay.**" Adrian

❸ Growing strong roots

From the little seed of a group, Freedom grew stronger. It needed money to be able to meet the ambitions of its founders.

It needed more resources than its team of dedicated sessional workers. The Management Committee decided to apply for funding from the National Lottery Charities Board.

The National Lottery was launched by Prime Minister John Major in November 1994. 28% of the profits from the Lottery was 'devoted to good causes': in its first year £267m of lottery money went to the good causes – charity, arts, heritage, sports, millennium projects, with £154m going to charities. It brought about a significant change in the funding opportunities for small groups such as Freedom. At a very early stage in its life, the merged group decided to take a chance and apply for National Lottery Funding. The grant application was for £171,100, to cover three years' funding 'to co-ordinate effective service provision for lesbians and gay young people'.

"The only risk as far as we were concerned was the amount of time we'd have to spend to put the bid together. It took days of working to get it together. We were in the first round of lottery bids for young people." Adrian

It is hard now to capture what a daring act this was, especially for a new group which had not even become a registered charity when it put in the Lottery application. The funding would enable both growth and recognition for Freedom Youth, and would give the group unimaginable security to support this – at least for three years. Even posting the largely handwritten application form was memorable.

> *"We drove from the office to the Royal Mail building, where there was a post box. I can see in my mind's eye this A4 brown envelope, handwritten in blue ballpoint pen that we sent to the Lottery. And those of us in the car, putting our hands on the envelope and putting our wishes into it to wish it success."* Berkeley

And it was successful! On June 11th, 1996, Freedom issued a press release announcing the award. Committee Members were *"overjoyed when the news came through".*

> *"It was just incredible, it felt like winning the lottery, literally because all of us had such an emotional attachment to Freedom Youth in its early years. Up to then it was a struggle. The local authority just couldn't quite get the case and the health authority didn't quite have the money and everything was given in kind or was such small amounts of money that to suddenly have an organisation say, 'here's this huge investment' and we could create this full-time project, it was just incredible, unbelievable."* Berkeley

Not everyone was pleased. Nationally, there was some controversy about how lottery 'good causes' money was spent. On June 11th, 1996, the Independent newspaper reported that "John Major condemned the distribution of lottery money to charitable schemes for gay people, lesbians, deportees and prostitutes as 'ill-founded and ill-judged' yesterday, in an unprecedented attack on the grant-making process. Mr Major told the Commons that while he welcomed the grants to charities, a minority were inappropriate. 'A small number do not in my judgement reflect the way Parliament and the public expected lottery money to be spent.'" The Freedom Youth grant, which was one of the larger among the "controversial" recipients, was reported in the Bristol Evening Post and Western Daily Press. And on June 20th, the Daily Mail reported

Gay Barbecues To Burn Lottery Cash

A National Lottery Award of £160,000 to a homosexual youth group provoked outrage yesterday. Freedom Youth will use the windfall to fund 'social activities' including summer barbecues. David Wilshire, Tory MP for Spelthorne, said the award was 'absolutely disgraceful'. Michael Roe, the Tory Prospective Parliamentary candidate for Bristol South said 'this group is nothing more than a dating agency for young gays and lesbians.'

The National Lottery Charities Board defended its decision making, asserting that it awarded grants "on the basis of merit, not popularity." And, it said, "projects for gay people, lesbians and deportees accounted for less than one per cent of the total."

> *"The Lottery were amazing. We contacted their press office and said we're getting a huge amount of flak from local newspapers, and they said 'you have given us all the information we needed and we made the decision. It's not your job to defend whether you got the money or not, it's our job because we gave the funding to you.' They said that we shouldn't have to worry about it, and we should just pass on the hostile contacts to the Lottery press office."* Adrian

The Lottery funding enabled Freedom to develop from a sessional group into a full time project, with a full time development worker, an administrator and activity funding. This gave the workers *"more opportunity for people to prepare and plan and, and deliver really, whereas before, you know, we had a workers' meeting on the night, with a little bit of time to do some pre-planning. So I remember it as being positive."* Julia

By April 1997, Freedom's Management Committee had worked up a rigorous set of policies and procedures and had appointed Mo Hand, a full time Development Worker described in the 1996/7 Annual Report as "of the highest calibre...who built a supportive, informative and dynamic programme suited both to the needs and wants of the young people." It wasn't only the programme that was dynamic. As Helen Webster, Co-Chair of Freedom wrote in the first Annual Report:

> *"Much has happened over the past few years. It seems a long time ago that Susan Moores (BYLBG) and Adrian Murphy had the idea for a grand plan to have one big lesbian and gay youth project. It's been a lot of hard work by a lot of people, most of whom have given their time in a voluntary capacity, but the rewards are countless. For many of us involved there wasn't the support when and where we grew up, so to be a part of such a project is a proud feeling."*

The three years from 1996-1999, during which Freedom received Lottery funding, enabled it to put down strong roots. It gave the Management Committee considerable security which enabled a great deal of both courage and creativity in the work.

> *"Some of that should be attributed to the funding because without that sense of security you're distracted by struggling to find funding for this or funding for that and not just to provide a positive resource for the group."* Mitch

Freedom with funding

The Lottery grant allowed Freedom to build both its local credibility and its local presence. With a full time development worker supported by an administrator and sessional staff, Freedom was able to grow. John McVerry, Freedom's Co-Chair, wrote in the 1996/7 Annual Report that

> *"Every week sees new young people coming to Freedom. Our intent is that everyone one of them will build their lives with confidence in their abilities, secure in the validity of their sexual orientation and with an uncrushable sense of their own self-worth."*

That Annual Report tells us that in the first 15 months of the Lottery funding, Freedom had "made contact with about 200 young people from Bristol, South Gloucestershire, North Somerset and Bath." It started running four sessions a week: the Tuesday evening Drop-In, a Coming Out Group, a Young Women's Group and a Young Men's Group. In 1998, funding was secured from Bath and North East Somerset Council to support a group in Bath as well. Numbers continued to grow.

Even so, finding Freedom wasn't always easy. In 1996, hardly anyone used the internet and it was still at least 10 years before Facebook would become widely used. Many young people still found out about Freedom through word of mouth and some young people found the group through leaflets. Others were referred by different agencies. Some found their way to Freedom because of the bad press that the group still received, which Babs described as "advertising for the group."

> *"The Evening Post ran a very negative article about Freedom. But the problem was we got 30 new young people arrive in the two weeks following it. And then about six months later they did*

35

What brought you to Freedom?

- other people I know that come here
- wanted to meet gay people
- putting something back into the gay community
- keeping up with old friends and making new ones
- peer pressure
- support
- people are on the same wavelength
- isolated and lonely
- seeking sanity and sanctuary
- to find my identity

Consultation with Freedom members 1998

another one and we got another influx. We got so many young people that we couldn't cope with the number of new members – more than 50 people arrived in one night. So we wrote to the Evening Post to ask them if they would please stop writing articles about Freedom because 'every time you write an article we get huge numbers of young people turning up.' They never wrote another article about us again." Adrian

Fun with funding

The three years of Lottery funding enabled a wide ranging programme. Leighton recalled doing *"a lot of fun things"* in the Tuesday evening drop ins. Rachel remembered *"making pumpkin ice cream at Halloween."* There were days out,

"A picnic up at the Observatory, sports days and games and every

once in a while we all went to the Shilling afterwards which was always fun." Leighton

The Annual Reports list some of the workshops which were "a key part of Freedom's programme." Some were educative and/or political, such as anti-racism, lesbian and gay rights, homelessness, drugs awareness, sexual health, relationships, transgender issues, lesbian parenting and ageism. Some were aimed at supporting young people to move towards independence, such as self defence, surfing the net or cooking on a budget. And some were more social, cultural or fun. There were arts and crafts sessions, cultural evenings, and shiatsu, meditation and creative writing workshops.

The staff organised three residential weekends in rural Wales in 1997, the first for the Young Women's Group, and the second for the Young Men's Group. The third weekend was organised in partnership with a lesbian and gay youth project in Swindon. The theme was challenging racism. The Annual Report 1996/7 says that "this event coincided with the European Year Against Racism and enabled participants to explore issues of multi-oppression and develop strategies for positive change."

Another three residential weekends were organised in 1998. One was a peer education weekend. The Young Men's weekend was organised with Aled Richards Trust and included learning self-defence and assertiveness skills. The Young Women's Residential was in celebration of International Women's Day. Nine young women and four staff went to Wales. *"It was cool,"* according to a write up in the Freedom Newsletter. There were workshops, walks, visits to local pubs (one hostile, one welcoming).

The residential weekends offered *"A safe space where I could express my feeling I can't express in everyday life"* and enabled workers to get to know Freedom members better and to understand their concerns and their needs. Many of the young people said that these events helped to increase their confidence and self-esteem. One of the young women who went to the 1998 weekend wrote

Freedom Youth Programme: June 1998

Monday	1st		Coming out Group (Mixed)
Tuesday	2	Drop in	Members meeting – Arts & Crafts
Thursday	4	YMG*	Sexuality Roadshow sketches
Saturday	6	YWG**	Picnic and Softball (bring food to share)
Monday	8		Coming out Group (Mixed)
Tuesday	9	Drop in	Chill-Out Zone
Thursday	11	YMG	Practical ways of combatting Homophobia
Saturday	13	YWG	Mental health debate
Monday	15		Coming out Group (Mixed)
Tuesday	16	Drop in	Creative writing workshop
Thursday	18	YMG	Member led workshop on homelessness with Leon
Saturday	20	YWG	Member led workshop on sex and sexuality
Monday	22		Coming out Group (Mixed)
Tuesday	23	Drop in	Discussion on alcohol in the lesbian & gay community
Thursday	25	YMG	Theatre/film night
Saturday	27	YWG	Sports Day (wear trainers/pumps)

*YMG = Young Men's Group   **YWG = Young Women's Group

that *"I liked that we all got on really well. It wasn't an us and them situation between the members and the workers. I also enjoyed hugging trees."* An evaluation of the 1998 young women's weekend reported that *"while overall, it was all about fun,"* young women reported that they came away from the weekend with a greater awareness of their own skills, including finding that *"I am good at team work and communication"* and *"I can cook, for large groups".* And that *"I've got a lot to learn!"*

Back at Freedom's weekly sessions, activities included drama and role play. In 1998, members worked on the Sexuality Road Show through which they explored their own identities, and how society can respond. It was performed at the Create Centre in front of the programme sponsors. Freedom members reported, in the 1998 Annual Report, that

"The performance included a lesbian rap, a sketch on men's body image and a really funny parliament scene. Both the performers

and the audience enjoyed it."

"It was exciting to be a part of Freedom. We used creativity to capture the skills of young people. A lot of them felt passionate about the fact that this was the only space where they felt safe."
Mitch

This helped the workers and the young people to explore both their creativity and their identities.

In 1997, Freedom developed a training programme for organisations "wishing to look at issues effecting lesbian and gay youth." By 1999, it had also established a partnership with East Bristol Youth Housing through which two houses had been secured which offered housing and support for LGB young people who were facing homelessness, usually because they were not able to remain in their family home.

Freedom set up a Peer Education Programme for members. In the first year, the focus of the project was on training for peer educators, and working with them to define this role, its boundaries, and what the project might do. The group of peer educators then ran regular member-led workshops at some of the Freedom sessions. They also participated in conferences and events locally, such as Bristol Pride and International Women's Day, and in the Youth Clubs UK National Conference 1997. Members wrote in the 1996/7 Annual Report

"Initially none of us had a clue what this was all about, but with appropriate training we are eventually getting the hang of it."

The following year, they reported

"We've taken more responsibility for how the programme is run and our member-led sessions in mental health, sexual health and relationships were very popular. Since our 'peer education weekend' we have learnt a lot more about how to facilitate sessions for the group."

By 1999, there was a core group of 11 peer educators who carried out work within Freedom as well as in local schools.

Highly Visible – and infamous

The amount and quality of activity during this period gave Freedom Youth a strong local presence and a great deal of credibility. It was able to attract further funding for two media based projects, 'Beyond a Phase' and 'Under Exposed'.

'Beyond a Phase' was a simple teaching pack which gained notoriety, and became somewhat infamous. It had two parts: a 14-minute video and booklet for teachers. The materials were written and produced by Freedom Youth, and the pack was paid for by Health Promotion Service Avon and went out under their name. 'Beyond a Phase' aimed to challenge heterosexism and to enable the development of a discussion on issues of sexuality in the classroom. The rationale for this resource was explained in the introduction:

"Every day we hear name-calling echoing down the corridors of our schools. We can certainly sense the pain and humiliation of the young people and sometimes we can see their anger. This teaching pack is designed not only to give teachers many valuable resources, but also to provide practical suggestions for helping to reduce homophobia in our schools."

The video is entirely made up of interviews with Freedom members. It explores their experiences, and the impact of homophobic bullying, oppression and the 'accepted norm' on their lives. The teachers' pack is made up of a series of exercises. 'Beyond a Phase' was bought, according to the Sunday Times, by 180 schools nationally. Locally, Freedom workers went into schools to run sessions based on the pack. With Section 28 still on the statute books, this wasn't straightforward, and took some courage.

'Beyond a Phase'

A Practical Guide to Challenging Homophobia in Schools

Produced by Health Promotion Service Avon

TEACHERS' PACK

The 1999 Annual Report tells us that "The teaching pack has generated much media attention in both the local and national press." Which is a very understated way of saying that in some parts of the media, and in some political arenas, it was seen as scandalous.

An article in the Sunday Times, January 30th, 2000 by Rosie Waterhouse and James Clark screamed

UK School Video Tells Children To Try Gay Sex

"A video that encourages schoolchildren as young as 14 to experiment with gay sex has caused outrage among MPs and family campaigners. The film, now available in 180 schools, also asks pupils aged 14-16 to discuss whether a fictional 15-year-old boy – Michael – should have unprotected gay sex with his boyfriend."

Well, it doesn't… but that didn't stop campaigners citing it "as a prime example of why Labour should abandon plans to scrap section 28" (Sunday Times). One such campaign group was the Edinburgh-based Christian Institute which produced a widely promoted pamphlet in January 2000 called "The Case for Keeping Section 28: protection from manipulation." This pamphlet devoted a full page to Freedom's resource pack. It reported with horror that 'Beyond a Phase' was bought by both Fife Education Authority and a school in Inverness. It acknowledged that

> *"Of course, there is no legal requirement upon councils or schools to notify parents of the use of such material. However, in theory Section 28 should stop Fife actually using this material with children in schools."*

In horrified tones, the Christian Institute tells us why. The video, it says, "encourages school children as young as 13 to experiment with same-sex partners." It claims that the teaching pack offers an

Spot the Heterosexual

exercise which asks students to consider other people's feelings and realities by posing "scenarios in which pupils are required to imagine themselves…" meeting or being friends with someone who is questioning their sexuality. A humorous exercise to "Spot the Heterosexual" was emblazoned across the pages of The Scotsman newspaper (11 November 1999) and reproduced in the Christian Institute publication. The Christian Institute was horrified that amongst the skills which the teaching pack sought to give to children were the abilities to "cope with 'coming out' and questioning one's sexuality and making positive sexual choices."

Which you could say makes a very convincing case for the need for the teaching pack. But that view wasn't shared by its detractors. According to the Sunday Times article,

> "Valerie Riches, of the Family and Youth Campaign pressure group, said: 'This puts concepts and activities into the minds of youngsters they would not normally think about.' Last night Liam Fox, the Conservative health spokesman, said few parents would want their children 'exposed' to the film and said he would demand that the Department of Health investigate."

Health Promotion Services Avon defended 'Beyond a Phase', arguing that "the video and teachers pack promotes the values of tolerance and understanding and that everyone has a right to be accepted whatever their sexuality" and that it "treats a difficult subject with great sensitivity. Local teachers consider it a valuable resource and we fully support its use in schools."

In time, 'Beyond a Phase' would come to be seen as an example of good practice in addressing sexuality in schools. But that didn't stop it from being cited in a House of Lords debate on April 3, 2003, when Baroness Blatch once again misquoted from it and called it one of the "inappropriate materials" that local authorities were "peddling" in schools. It was, she said, a reason to oppose the repeal of Section 28.

Under Exposed

Freedom's photography project, 'Under Exposed', on the other hand, received far less attention. Freedom worked with the Watershed Media Centre in Bristol and had financial support from Bristol City Council for this project. Young people produced a 'positive image calendar for 1999' to challenge negative stereotypes and to challenge the impacts of homophobia. They produced positive images in a calendar along with a set of post cards that highlighted the experience of young people who were questioning their sexuality. The 1999 Annual Report says that all of the young people involved "felt passionately about this piece of work. Most had direct experience of homophobia and through participating in the project were able to share and channel their experiences in a safe setting with a view to raising public awareness."

For the young people involved, it was exciting, inspiring, and hard work.

"I'm not sure that any of us knew what to expect when we arrived at the Watershed on the first day of our course. With only two weeks to learn how to use the camera, set up a studio, develop negatives and prints, and to navigate through Photoshop – the learning curve was very steep, but by week two we looked like professionals. By the second Thursday it had all started to come together and the first page layouts were ready. I don't think any of us realised how much we could achieve in only two weeks and the experience was one that we won't forget in a hurry. Many thanks to the tutors, Ruth and Suzanne, and to the Watershed for the use of the facilities." (Hannah, member, in 1998 Annual Report)

It's easy to forget how few positive images there were of LGB young people in the late 1990s. And how, without access to the internet, it was very difficult to find what little there was. So 'Under Exposed' and 'Beyond a Phase' were vital affirmations of young people's experiences, both within Freedom Youth and beyond.

Freedom 1999: firmly rooted

The three years during which Freedom was well funded gave the group a high level of independence which enabled a very wide range of activities, including campaigning and political awareness raising. As the members wrote in the 1999 Annual Report:

> "Of course, it hasn't all been fun. As a group we have been very active in campaigning for an equal age of consent, and the abolition of the dreaded Section 28. This included letter writing, lobbying our MPs and a day trip to Parliament."

With Lottery funding, Freedom Youth gained the stability to grow. It was able to support an ever increasing number of young people. By producing resources that hadn't existed anywhere before, Freedom was able to reach young people who didn't live in Bristol or couldn't come to any of its sessions. It enabled many young people to come to terms with their sexuality. *"Nowadays, that might not seem like a big deal. But in the climate of Section 28, it was a tall order. We saved lives. We were working with a number of young people with para-suicidal behaviour; and they survived."* (Mo)

The partnership which built Freedom Youth had good networks in Bristol, and used them to invite speakers to the Tuesday night Drop Ins. At one session a senior Police Inspector came in and gave a talk. This session in particular helped to give young people a feeling that they would be safer, both inside and outside of Freedom.

> "Back then we didn't have a lot of legal protection, we didn't really understand where we stood, and we feared the police. Because of the age of consent, you weren't even allowed in the clubs until you were 21 and you didn't feel safe around the police. You heard or read all the horror stories in the newspapers and LGB press, these horror stories about police raiding gay venues.

So having someone who was funny, engaging and really friendly, it led to the feeling that the police were actually looking out for you." Leighton

The case for safe spaces

Freedom was strong. It was visible. And every week, more young people came to its sessions. This helped to make the case for specialist provision within the youth service. Nationally and locally, there was a realisation that LGB young people needed support.

"Homophobia was rife in all the mainstream youth clubs I worked in. There was always some degree of bullying so Freedom offered something that a lot of mainstream youth groups didn't offer: specific work around the experiences that young LGB people were having. It offered the only space for young people to reduce the isolation." Babs

"The sad statistics about the impact of homophobia on young people were partly what drove lesbian and gay youth workers to feel that this is an absolute need." Mitch

As Adrian said, there was a passion for this among the workers and committee members. The commitment that has kept Freedom Youth running continuously from 1995-2016 is deeply rooted in both personal understanding and experience along with professional knowledge.

"One of the reasons I got involved in LGB youth work was because I was a lesbian in the 70s. I couldn't come out. You know, the amount of abuse. There were no support groups. We should always remember the struggle that people have had over the years." Babs

"Remembering how it felt as a young Catholic boy growing up in Hartcliffe, in the 70s as a teenager. I didn't want anyone to go through that loneliness and having nowhere to go and having no one to talk to about how you felt and your sexuality and they weren't going to go back and tell your mum within minutes of you talking about it…" Adrian

Even today, *"My motivation for working at Freedom is to create a space that I didn't have."* Henry

Freedom has always argued that it's important that LGBT provision is run mainly by LGBT workers. If you never see anyone 'like yourself' how do you know what you want to be or how to be that as you grow up differently?

"There was always a need for the groups to be run by LGBT staff to give a positive identity. For workers who were in the adult world, who can understand how hard this might be for me, who have had those experiences as well." Mitch

Sue would explain to other parents who contacted the 'Families and Friends of Lesbians and Gays' (FFLAG) helpline that the workers were LGB (and later LGBT) adults who were also professionally trained – a fact that surprised some parents who were struggling with their children's sexuality/identity.

"'Well they have to be' I said. 'You can't have straight people running a youth group for gay people. They don't know what it's like to be gay. How could they sit and have a one-to-one if they don't know what it's like?'. I can have a one-to-one with other parents because we know what it's like to have a gay child. But I couldn't run a group because I don't know what it's like to be gay." Sue

Frederick, Geo and Rosa in conversation, about the Freedom workers

"I still wish I did have a group like Freedom to go to. I wish I had somewhere to go to every week and just kind of complain about my problems to a nice youth worker. Cos they're so trusted. They are trusted adult LGBT role models. And there's also this feeling that they've got your best interest at heart. They haven't got some ulterior motive. They are there for you, not like other people who might have their own reasons for the advice they give you. They understand you. No one my age that I knew understood what I was going through. And we felt that they were learning from young people."

With the stability of the Lottery funding, the workers learned a great deal about young people's needs and how to address them, and shared their growing understanding with other professionals working with young people. This stood Freedom in good stead in the years that followed.

> *"Some very good work came out of those three years that I think helped the local authorities to see the importance of Freedom."*
> Julia

But all good things, including Lottery grants, come to an end. Funding for the full-time post ran out and Mo Hand left in March 1999. Freedom was run, once again, by sessional workers. Initially, Mitch McMorrow took on running the groups and Babs McPhail provided supervision. Both remained committed to Freedom Youth, and their input along with the dedication of the Management Committee enabled Freedom to carry on. Once again, Freedom's activity focused on maintaining the Tuesday evening sessions. Often these were run by Management Committee members, many of whom were highly experienced youth workers. The Committee shrunk in size while its workload increased. Lesley Mansell, Co-Chair of Freedom wrote in the Annual Report in 1999 "the biggest task for the management committee is to find more funding to continue this valuable work."

There's a community out there:

With people who are just like me

Freedom was five years old in the millennium year. Things were changing for the better but it was still tough to be out and many young people felt very isolated, whether they were in or out and no matter how comfortable they were with their identity.

In 2000 the Labour government introduced legislation to scrap Section 28, but this was defeated by a House of Lords campaign led by Baroness Young. The government succeeded in passing a law to lift the ban on lesbians and gay men serving in the Armed Forces. In 2001 the age of consent for gay men was lowered to 16, making it the same as the age of consent for straight people. On the political front, there was greater acceptance of LGB people and issues. And a few more of us were in the public eye.

In 1997 Labour's Stephen Twigg became the first openly gay politician to be elected to the House of Commons. Angela Eagle, Labour MP for Wallasey near Liverpool, came out. So did Ellen DeGeneres who had a popular sitcom on TV which, despite its popularity and high ratings, was cancelled at the end of the 1997 season. In 1999 Michael Cashman, an openly gay former EastEnders star, was elected to the European Parliament. In 2002 Will Young, winner of the first Pop Idol, came out. In the same year, Brian

Dowling became the first openly gay children's TV presenter in the UK on SMTV Live.

But LGB people were still invisible in everyday life. Many of us try not to stand out in the crowd, because we know that this isn't always the route to an easy, happy or safe life. Invisibility has always made it tough for many young people just to walk through the door. As Henry said, *"Everyone's had a first session."*

"The first time I turned up at Freedom, I was super-nervous. I didn't know what to expect. I had only ever met anybody who identified in the LGBTQ spectrum at my college and that was only a couple of us… so really I was very nervous. But the minute I got there everyone was so welcoming." Vicci

"I was shaking like a leaf, I was so nervous, walked in and Berkeley pulled me aside and had a chat with me and calmed me down, made me a cup of tea and everybody was really friendly and said 'oh hi, how you doing' and that was kind of it for the first session. After that, I met loads of people, it was absolutely fantastic, and I felt so relieved just to find other people of my own age." Paul

once there…

"I did feel they'd made an effort to include me. It felt safer than the other attempts that I'd made to meet people in Bristol" Rachel

With people who are just like me

Freedom Youth has always been more than a support group. It's always been a place where young people have been able to build friendships and community. So many people who spoke or wrote about Freedom Youth as part of this project said that they didn't know any other LGBT people, of any age, before Freedom.

How did you feel during your first few sessions of Freedom?

- free, understood, accepted
- I was made to feel at home and confident in Freedom, a supportive environment
- shy, but I made good friends fast
- nervous, couldn't speak, shy but relieved to have found other people my own age
- nervous but everyone was lovely
- scared, nervous, then I felt involved
- nervous, but comfortable to express myself which was amazing!

From a survey carried out for 'Free to be me'

"It was an opportunity to meet other gay people, there was a lot of social exclusion at the time so the support of other gay, lesbian and bisexual people was really important. It gave you a kind of solidarity and a feeling of mutual support when there was so much oppression around you. The age of consent was different then, particularly for gay men. Inequality was definitely very significant. I enjoyed an active social life but through Freedom I developed a wide network of friends and that really increased my confidence and my acceptance of who I was." Scott

Whether your family knew or didn't know, or was supportive or not.

"It was just a really nice way to meet other gay teenagers. Even though the school I went to was quite accepting, my family was

accepting there was nobody else really I knew who was growing up gay." Max

"Meeting other like-minded people," gives young people a lot of confidence. So, it's not surprising that for many, Freedom has become "the highlight of their week, their main social event, the place where their friends are." Hannah

"I've really close friendships with a lot of the people in Freedom. They're really good to talk to if I've got any worries, I can talk to people there. It's a nice social space where I can have a good time. And it's a secure structure, whatever's happened during the week it's always there…" Rosa

So, Freedom members know it as a place

"That people can go and feel that there are friends and allies who will care for them and support them and be interested in them no matter where they're up to in their gender and sexuality journey." Henry

For Freedom workers, it has always been joyful to see

"Young people looking happy, feeling like they had somewhere where they could share their story and they express themselves and feel like they could make real strong networks of friends." Mitch

Freedom is family

Some young people told their parents they were going 'anyplace else' than an LGBT youth group on a Tuesday evening. Some people said it took months after gaining the support of the Freedom family to have the confidence to come out at home. Even now, in 2016, some people's families don't know where they go on a Tuesday evening and some actively oppose young people going to Freedom Youth. But, in the group, everyone is accepted for who they are.

"There's a lot of recreating family in Freedom. There's that language around, 'we're all a family'. We all look for that. But it's more pertinent and poignant I think when maybe your family aren't accepting of you." Henry

"A lot of people in Freedom call it their family because even today not all families accept people, or they only grudgingly accept them as they are. Or they make LGBT young people feel that they have to make an effort to be accepted" Rosa

Just as in families, there are disagreements… but working out how to resolve them is an invaluable life lesson for everyone.

"The world isn't going to be that perfect, there's always going to be someone who has a problem with something. In Freedom, even if you have a different opinion to someone, they're going to accept you have that opinion. People argue." Rosa

"And some members have really annoyed me. But, we all have those moments, that's family. In your own family you're going to have moments. You're all going to argue, but it'll work out with people who are going to appreciate you for you. That's the best thing about Freedom." Frederick

This is so often the case with LGBT groups. Why else is the song "We are Family" always one of the Top Ten LGBT Anthems?

Freedom: a gateway to the wider community

Since 1995, Freedom has helped young people to grow in confidence, and to move on out into their own lives. It has given LGBT young people another safety net which society often fails to do. Young people have gained a *"group of people who are on my side"* (Rosa). Freedom workers have acted as role models who are *"older than me, who understand my lifestyle, where I'm living and my education situation. That makes a big difference."* (Leighton).

And Freedom has enabled members to connect to the wider and more diverse LGBT community.

"I made loads of new friends and it was the first time I'd had a community behind me which let me safely explore the scene for the first time. Within a couple of weeks, I was going to the more well-known clubs with some of the people that I'd made friends with." Thom

"Going to the pub, the Queenshilling. We'd go en masse after Freedom closed, we'd probably have five or six tables, and so we had a real presence there. For many of them, it was the first time they'd been able to go to a gay pub. That was really powerful. They didn't feel intimidated. They didn't feel that they needed to have much money because they were there with a big group, and they felt part of it because they were members of Freedom." Adrian

This sense of connectedness to the wider LGBT community was particularly strong when Freedom went to Pride. In London, in Cardiff, and in Bristol.

"Seeing the Freedom flag at Pride for the first time, getting a group of young people going to Pride, that was a really lovely moment." Berkeley

Freedom members on the Bristol Pride March 2015

"We always went to Pride events. We always went to rallies. The voice of LGBT young people in Bristol was very strong." Babs

Many young people would not have gone on their own. Going together as a group gave a sense of safety to young people, and increased their feelings about being part of the rainbow community.

"You get to walk in Bristol Pride or a bigger Pride, any Pride. You get be a part of it and to be there with the whole community, feeling like you have a place where people are going to accept you. This is so, so important for young people." Geo

It gives people a *"kind of community feel, outside of Freedom, as well as being inside Freedom"* (Thom). Which is important because

"Somewhere like Pride is so visible and it's such a big party, such a big celebration of who we are in all our diversity that for young people to attend Pride is a stepping up of their confidence. A way of recognising that they are part of a big community of people who have had similar experiences to them and can relate to them. So coming to Pride, gaining confidence and being their joyful selves at those sort of celebrations is just fantastic." Mitch

⑤ What Freedom did next

The legal situation for LGBT people continued to improve. Section 28 was finally repealed. But Freedom faced a difficult and uncertain future.

The early 2000s saw real changes in the position of LGBT people in both the law and in society. In 2002 equal rights were granted to same sex couples applying to adopt children. In 2003 a new law came into force protecting LGBT people from discrimination at work. In 2004 the Civil Partnership Act was passed, giving same-sex couples the same legal rights as married couples. In the same year the Gender Recognition Act was passed, allowing trans people to change their legal gender.

And in 2003 Section 28 was finally repealed. Sir Ian McKellen, who had campaigned actively against this law, said that "if Section 28 and the attitudes behind it had remained then society would still believe that gay people are second-class citizens and that it is right that they should be treated as second class citizens."

Back at Freedom, young people kept coming through the doors. The Annual Report described how "1999 saw an increase in youth membership, with young women making up 40% of the membership, compared to 10% in 1997. Users experiencing mental health issues make up 50% of the current membership." But while demand increased, the funding didn't. The Lottery grant had run out, and the Management Committee had ever decreasing resources to meet the growing needs of LGBT young people in Bristol and the surrounding area.

Freedom had some relatively small grants from the four local authorities which had previously made up Avon County

- Bristol: £6,001
- Bath and North East Somerset: £1,868
- North Somerset: £1,125
- South Gloucestershire: £1,094

By 2001, it was back to running a skeleton service on Tuesday evenings. Lesley Mansell, Co-Chair, wrote in the 2001 Annual Report that *"The year 2001 saw Freedom Youth just about keeping its head above water."* The Management Committee had shrunk to five members. They discussed what to do, including the possibility of having to close. One option was to merge with Terence Higgins Trust but the management committee decided not to do this. They wanted to maintain the strong youth work focus, and said that THT was not a "main provider of youth services".

The commitment to maintain Freedom Youth was strong. Many of the early members of both BYLBG and Freedom remained dedicated to the group and continued to support it with passion, energy and creativity. New staff were recruited to run the Tuesday night sessions from August 2001. Babs supervised and supported the staff team. Susan Moores, who had been instrumental in setting up BYLBG, became the "Temporary Leader in Charge". Her reports to the Management Committee describe a "core group of 10 young people, rising to 18 some weeks" between November 2001 and March 2002. Sessional staff ran the Tuesday night sessions, and worked with young people on specific additional projects including a short film idea on homophobic bullying.

The Annual Report in 2001 states that "Freedom Youth remains a

Young People's Annual Report, 2001: What we have enjoyed:

- Pancake night: horrible pancakes which we all had a go at cooking from a shop bought mixture. They were really bad and we made a right mess, but we laughed a lot and got to know some of the new members better.

- Lesbian and Gay Parenting issues workshop: this was so interesting that we asked the facilitator to come back and tell us more about it. We learned about the law around partnerships and parenting and talked about our own families and how we felt about the prospect of being parents in the future.

- CD-ROM workshop on 'coming out for young women. We volunteered for this and got paid because all our stories went to help make a CD-ROM about how it feels to be gay/bisexual in school, with families and with your friends. The workshop was facilitated by a researcher from London. She was really good at supporting us to tell our stories in our own way.

- Gay and Lesbian Legislation. We enjoyed this because it was a workshop we had asked for and the facilitator was really good at talking about her own experience and in getting us to express our feelings about how the law is at the moment and how we think it should be.

- Mardi Gras. This was an excellent day trip to London. We met up with youth groups from around the country and did the parade on a float.... We were given costumes which we each

customised so that they expressed something about our personalities. It was a long day and we were all exhausted by the time we got home but we had a great time.

- Quasar – lasar quest

- Sexual health workshop... This was a fun and safe way to talk about the risks involved in sex and to learn ways to make sure we stay as safe as possible.

- Yoga Workshop

- Batik, silk painting and tie-die workshop

- We also enjoyed the 'chill out nights' as they gave us the opportunity to get to know each other and just 'hang out'...

- Writing things for the 'Newsletter'. We enjoyed this as it lets people know what we do at Freedom and about how we see the world.

- Move-on group. We decided to set up a group for older people who use Freedom to help us move on from using the group. We haven't decided on a name, but it might be 'the Free Radicals' or 'Freedom Plus'. This group is going to be run by Freedom members and supported by a member of the Youth Work Team... We have very much enjoyed making all the decisions about the group.

- Freedom being open.... It has given us a safe place to meet other young people, and it's been good to have staff on hand if we need advice and information or support at any time.

If you are lesbian, gay or bisexual,
or unsure about your sexuality and need
support with issues that affect your life, then

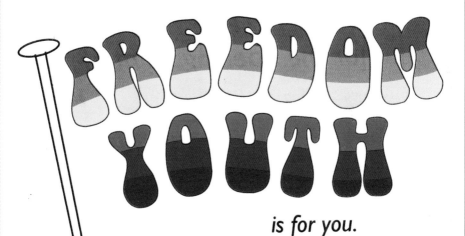

is for you.

FREEDOM YOUTH offers:

▼ a safe space for you to meet other people

▼ a chance to look at issues that affect you,
including coming out and safer sex

▼ activities, information, refreshments,
friendship and fun

For more information, contact
Berkeley on (0117) 955 1000

Supported by: Gay Mens' Project, Aled Richards Trust, CASCADE,
Bristol Young Lesbian and Bisexual Group, Bristol Lesbian and Gay Switchboard,
Bristol Area Specialist Health Promotion Service

The first Freedom leaflet, 1996

Freedom

0117 9553355

Before Freedom I was all alone.
I didn't have anyone to talk to
about my feelings. Attending
Freedom has given me a
stronger identity and an
opportunity to meet others
who feel like me.

Freedom is
my weekly
escape from
the heterosexual
world where
I can feel
at home
and be open
about my
sexuality.

Freedom is a
great way to
meet people of
a similar age.
The atmosphere
is always
relaxed and
friendly. When
I'm not feeling
particularly
good about
myself and my
life, Freedom
seems the best
place to go.

Freedom
is my
lifeline.

Freedom Annual Report 1996/97

For a few hours each week
Freedom allows me to be myself.

Funded by

NATIONAL LOTTERY CHARITIES BOARD

HOMO...

...sexual?
...phobic?
...SAPIENS!

Top: Freedom Youth members and workers (Babs and Mitch) at an Outdoors Activity event.
Bottom: Post Card designed and produced as part of Under Exposed, 1998. (See page 46)

Want to be a world leader for the day?

Simulation Commonwealth Heads of Government Meeting in Bristol

HIV/AIDS, international security and terrorism, fair trade and the global warming are just some of the issues to be discussed by over 150 young people at the first ever Bristol Youth Commonwealth Heads Of Government Meeting

Friday 19 November 2004 at Bristol Council House

The Royal Commonwealth Society in partnership with Bristol City Council Young Peoples Services

For more information contact Stuart Smith, Bristol City Council Young Peoples Services
Tel: 0117 377 3673. Email: stuart smith@bristol-city.gov.uk

Home Office
BUILDING A SAFE, JUST
AND TOLERANT SOCIETY

department for
education and skills

Freedom participated in the Commonwealth Youth Heads of Government meeting in Bristol as part of its campaigning work.

HOMOPHOBIA HURTS

You are not alone

**IN 1997, 82% OF TEACHERS WERE AWARE OF
HOMOPHOBIC BULLYING,
YET ONLY 6% OF SCHOOLS HAD AN ANTI-BULLYING POLICY
WHICH INCLUDED LESBIAN AND GAY ABUSE.***

***Institute of Education**

LET'S CHANGE THIS!

Post Card designed and produced as part of Under Exposed, 1998. (See page 46)

Top: Freedom members and workers on their way to Cardiff Pride, 2005
Bottom: Skern Lodge residential, 2006

Young People's Services

Staff Development & Curriculum Unit

This calendar was designed by young people at Freedom Youth http://www.freedomyouth.co.uk/

N

What's Coming Up Next?

September 06 - August 07

2006

August

6-12 Sexual Health Week

12 International Youth Day

13-19 Bristol Mardi Gras Festival + Fringe

30 International Day of the Disappeared

7-14 National Transplant Week

July

2-8 G-week A national celebration of giving in schools.

June

2-8 Alzheimer's Awareness Week

14 World Blood Donor Day

20 World Refugee Day

29 Wrong Trousers Day

September

8 International Literacy Day

9 World First Aid Day

21 International Day of Peace

15-17 Clean Up the World Weekend

5 National Poetry Day

23-30 Leukaemia Research Awareness Week

10 World Mental Health Day

20-26 Islam Awareness Week

October

1-31 Black History Month

2-8 WOW (World Orphan Week)

1-7 Youth Work Week

6 World Smile Day

9 International Day against Fascism and Anti-semitism

6-12 Dyslexia Awareness Week

20-24 Anti-Bullying Week

November

May

1 May Day

17 International day against homophobia (IDAHO)

29 International Dance Day

25 Africa Malaria Day

1 World Asthma Day

April

23-29 International TV Turnoff Week

March

12 World Fair Trade Day

14 No Smoking Day

8 International Women's Day

25 Abolition 200 200 years ago slave trade was abolished in the British Empire (Events throughout the year.)

1 Self-Injury Awareness Day

February

18 International Migrants Day

31 Bug Busting Day: Head Lice Beware!

21 International Mother Language Day

4-10 Eating Disorders Awareness Week

1-28 LGBT History Month

December

3 International Day of Disabled Persons

10 Human Rights Day

27 Holocaust Memorial Day

1-31 Children's Cancer Month

1 World Aids Day

22-26 Cancertalk Week

January

Religious holidays - September 2006: 22-24th Rosh Hashanah (Jewish); **October:** 24th Sept - 23rd Oct Ramadan (Islam); 2nd Dasera (Hindu); 2nd Yom Kippur (Jewish); 14th Shemini Atzeret (Jewish); 15th Simchat Torah (Jewish); 20th Birth of the B'ab (Baha'i); 21st Diwali (Deepavali) (Hindu); 22nd Narka-Chaturdashi (Hindu); 24th Eid al Fitr - end of Ramadan (Islam); 31st All Hallows Eve (Christian); 31st Samhain (Pagan); **November:** 5th Guru Nanak Dev birthday (Sikh); 12th Birth of Baha'u'llah (Baha'i); 24th Guru Tegh Bahadur Martyrdom (Sikh); **December:** 25th Christmas (Christian); 31st Eid-al-Adha (Islam); **January 2007:** 5th Birth of Guru Gobind Singh Ji (Sikh); 7th Christmas (Eastern Orthodox); 29th Aashura (Islam); **February:** 16th Maha Shivaratri (Hinduism); 18th Lunar New Year / Chinese New Year (Buddhism, Confucianism); **March:** 4th Holi (Hinduism); 20th Malid-an-Nabi (Islam); 21st Naw Ruz (New Year) (Baha'i, Zoroastrianism); **April:** 3rd-10th Pesah (Passover) (Jewish); 6th Good Friday (Christian); 6th Holy Friday (Eastern Orthodox); 7th Holy Saturday (Christian); 8th Easter (Christian); 8th Pascha (Eastern Orthodox); 13th Vaisakhi (Sikh); 21st Ridvan (First day) (Baha'i); 29th Ridvan (Ninth day) (Baha'i); **May:** 2nd Ridvan (Twelfth Day) (Baha'i); 22nd-23rd Shavuot (Jewish); 23rd Declaration of the Báb (Baha'i); 29th Ascension of Bahá'u'lláh (Baha'i); **June:** 16th The Martyrdom of Guru Arjan (Sikh); 21st Summer Solstice/Alban Hefin/ Litha (Pagan); 24th St John the Baptist (Catholic); **July:** 6th Dalai Lama Birthday (Buddhist); 9th Martyrdom of the Bab (Baha'i); 11th Asalha Puja Day (Dhamma Day) (Buddhist); 11th Guru Purnima (Hindu); **August:** 1st Lammas (Christian); 1st Lughnassadh (Lammas) (Pagan); 3rd Tisha B'av (Jewish); 4th Raksha Bandhan (Hindu); 6th Transfiguration of Our Lord (Christian); 15th Assumption of Blessed Virgin Mary (Catholic); 16th Krishna Janmaashtami (Hindu); 22nd Lailat al Miraj (Islam); 27th Ganesa Chaturthi (Hindu); 27th St Monica (Catholic);

For further info and more religious holidays, visit www.countmecalendar.info
For further details about this calendar please contact Maria Cassidy, Senior Training & Curriculum Worker - 0117 3773651

Bristol Young People Services Calendar: Freedom members contributed to the content

Top: Freedom Youth after learning a traditional fan dance, with Japanese young people and their teachers, 2008. (see p.70) Top: Freedom members and workers at the London Dungeon, 2011

Top: Freedom members with the rainbow flag, 2012
Bottom: Two members of Freedom meet some of the cast of the L Word at L Fest 2012

Top: A banner made by Freedom Youth for Bristol Pride 2014
Bottom: Freedom members on the Bristol Pride March 2015

Top: Freedom members at the Annual Barbecue, July 2015
Bottom: Freedom Youth on a trip to a local high wire course, 2015

Top: Freedom members celebrating Christmas Eve together, 2015

Bottom: A blindfolded team building exercise on a Freedom trip, October 2015

Top: At a session in 2015
Bottom: Freedom members and workers celebrating 20 years of Freedom Youth, September 2015

op: Freedom plays Crazy Golf on a trip, January 2016

Bottom: Stuart Milk (at the back) visited Freedom Youth as part of LGBT History Month 2016

GAY YOUTH

1969

THEY WERE PROUD THEN!

AND WE ARE PROUD NOW!

FREEDOM YOUTH

Welcomes lesbians, gay men, bisexual
and transgender young people and those
questioning their sexuality aged between
13 - 21 years

tel 0117 377 3677 / www.freedomyouth.co.uk

RESPECT DIFFERENCE

Posters designed by Freedom Youth, approx 2006-2010

PEOPLE **LAUGH** AT CARTOONS

BUT IN **REAL LIFE**

HOMOPHOBIC ATTACKS ARE NO LAUGHING MATTER

FREEDOM YOUTH

Welcomes lesbians, gay men, bisexual
and transgender young people and those
questioning their sexuality aged between
13 - 21 years

tel: 0117 377 3677

STAMP OUT BULLYING

www.freedomyouth.co.uk

designed by
enlight
designs art
enlightdesigns@googlemail.com

DO YOU THINK ANY OF THESE YOUNG PEOPLE ARE LESBIAN, GAY OR BISEXUAL?

WHY DOES IT MATTER?

Freedom Youth

Welcomes lesbians, gay men, bisexual and transgender young people and those questioning their sexuality aged between 13 - 21 years

RESPECT DIFFERENCE

designed by:
enlight

tel 0117 377 3677 / www.freedomyouth.co.uk

Top: Freedom logo and leaflet produced in 1996, thanks to Lottery funding
Bottom: Freedom logo approx. 2000

FREEDOM

Freedom logo, 2016

vibrant, unique and much needed project." As can be seen from the range of activities that took place during the year. This is an edited list – there was much more!

The local authorities continued with their financial and in kind support but with no resources for anything other than the Tuesday night sessions, it was difficult to keep going. In 2002, Mitch took on the role of Chair of the Management Committee and slowly, Freedom started to rebuild. The 2002 Annual Report comments that Freedom "has only managed to keep going through the dedication and commitment of a couple of people."

Babs recalls that

"In 2002 when I got a full time post with Bristol City Council as the senior youth and community worker for LGB young people, Freedom was going through a difficult stage. There was hardly anybody left on the management committee. The funding wasn't there, there was limited staffing, we were struggling, there's no doubt that unless there was a change it was going to close." Babs

Into Bristol City Council's Youth Service

The idea of moving Freedom Youth into Bristol City Council's Youth Service began. It was a difficult discussion.

"On the one hand you want to be independent, but on the other hand you want to keep going." Helen

Committee members were particularly concerned that this specialist provision would be incorporated into mainstream youth clubs and so lost. But there was an equal worry that Freedom Youth would have to close its doors. Babs worked with Freedom members, committee members, and managers of Bristol's Youth Service to ensure that Freedom Youth could carry on and develop as a separate entity.

Statement of the outcome of a meeting held on 15.01.05 by the Management Committee of Freedom

Freedom Youth was set up nearly 10 years ago with the sole aim to ensure high quality youth work provision for LGB young people.

As a voluntary organisation we currently deliver youth work through a weekly drop in session and associated projects and activities. Times have changed and Freedom Youth has reviewed the methods by which it meets its aims.

Given Bristol City Council Young People's Services clearly resourced commitment to LGB youth work, Freedom Youth believes that it is the right time for services to be placed within the local authority and/or other appropriate youth work organisations from 1 April 2005.

What remains unchanged is Freedom Youth's commitment to seeing that the needs of lesbian, gay and bisexual young people are met.

"Basically I had resources. I had funding for staffing so I approached the management committee and I said 'let me take Freedom Youth into Bristol City Council and I promise you that I will develop it, and I will look after it'. And that's what happened."
Babs

And so the charity, Freedom Youth, was wound up. Adrian described how *"With full-time funding coming from Bristol City Council and without the management of staff, the Committee was there in name only."* Its members agreed that *"We'd recreate it if we needed to. In 2006 I wrote the cheque to hand over the last of the money that we had to Young Bristol, another youth organisation that had similar*

Skern Lodge: two Freedom members enjoying the high poles: 2006

aims to us on the proviso that it was to support lesbian and gay youth work in the Bristol area."

Freedom Youth carried on, every Tuesday night. Still in the same venue. And once again with the resources to expand its programme and activities – from residentials to radio.

"Skern Lodge was an away weekend, or maybe longer, where we did everything from getting lost in the woods, on purpose, to climbing up very high poles and abseiling." Geo

Babs impressed everyone because *"There was no pole or high wire too high"* for her!

Within the Youth Service, Freedom Youth was seen as a very successful group that was an important service for young people in Bristol. The quality of its youth work was praised by Ofsted, the government body that inspects and regulates schools and all other services for children and young people. Ofsted recognition helped Freedom to achieve a high level of respect within the Youth Service. Professionals working in the mainstream of the Youth Service gained a better understanding of the specific needs of LGBT young people, and why a separate group was needed.

> "We were in so much demand that if I didn't have the backing of the youth service, I wouldn't have had the resources to maintain this level of activity." Babs

Freedom also connected with other organisations that were campaigning for change, particularly for LGBT young people.

The relationship with Bristol's Youth Service and their backing brought some great opportunities, including encounters with fame.

By 2010, it was OK to challenge homophobia in schools, and many had active programmes, or simply arranged activities, that aimed to do just this. On November 2010, 'This is Bristol' ran a story headlined

Anti-homophobia push in schools

One of the world's finest actors visited two Bristol schools to support a charity that tackles homophobic bullying. Lord of the Rings star Sir Ian McKellen, co-founder of the charity Stonewall, visited the City Academy in Lawrence Hill and Fairfield High School in Horfield. During his visits Sir Ian took part in school assemblies and chatted to staff, pupils and governors. He also met a group of young people from 'Freedom Youth' to talk about their experiences.

Freedom got in on the act because Babs was part of Bristol City Council's Challenging Homophobia Group which did a lot of work

Meeting Sir Ian McKellen. 2010

in schools and promoted Stonewall's 'education champions'. She managed to arrange for a group from Freedom to be present when Sir Ian, one of the education champions, was at Fairfield School. Her argument was that it would be fitting for him to meet the only LGBT youth group in Bristol as well.

> *"We were packed the night I broke the news to Freedom that we were going to meet Sir Ian McKellen. I don't think I'll ever forget their faces! The whole group wanted to be part of this. On the day, they talked to him, they got his autograph, Sir Ian McKellen spent ages with our members. His manager said 'Sir Ian, we have to go, we have a taxi to catch.' He said 'Book another taxi.' It was fantastic."* Babs

And the Council Youth Service connection brought about one of the most exciting events in Freedom Youth's history.

Freedom goes to Japan: 17–31 August 2008

One day in around 2006, Babs got an email from the head of Bristol's Youth Services, saying that Freedom Youth had been invited to go to Japan.

Why?! What for?!

The exchange was, we believe, the first of its kind to take place between the UK and Japan involving LGBT young people. It developed from a meeting between Kanako Otsuji, the first out lesbian politician in Japan, and a Bristol City Council officer. This meeting took place in Geneva at an International Lesbian and Gay Association (ILGA) conference. The Japanese delegation was very interested in the LGBT youth work taking place in Bristol and proposed setting up an exchange. The formal invitation was accepted by the Head of Service of Bristol Youth and Play Services and the Senior Youth and Community worker responsible for leading LGBT youth work in Bristol.

The idea behind the exchange was that "young people from the different countries could share their experiences, ideas, information and dreams to build greater awareness and explore ways forward for all involved" according to a report to Bristol City Council about the visit.

It was an absolutely amazing opportunity both for the members of Freedom Youth and for the young people they met in Japan. Babs recalls that the Japanese hosts were very interested in the fact that we had an LGBT youth group: there was no equivalent youth service in Japan, let alone a group specifically for LGBT young people. They wanted to know all about it.

So much so that the group was *"followed by cameramen from*

NHK, the Japan Broadcasting Company, and interviewed the entire time and filmed. It was made into a documentary." Geo

But how did it begin?

"So, one Tuesday evening Babs said 'OK, would anyone like to go to Japan?' And immediately everyone put their hands up and there's, there must have been about 25 of us there at the time. I'm there, elbowing my way to the front, thinking I can do this, I can do this." Geo

It was an expensive project and one that made big demands on the young people, and the youth workers, who went. The group had to work really hard to prepare for the trip: "It was a lot of work, we did probably a year's work in three months", meeting every week to plan the trip. As ambassadors for Freedom Youth, and for Bristol City Council, the group had to think about the messages and information they wanted to give, as well as what they wanted to get out of it themselves. They had to learn about Japanese customs, and to learn some of the language. They had to decide what workshops they wanted to run. They had training in how to do presentations and confidence building because group members would be addressing big audiences.

"Going to a country like Japan, the language barrier, the culture, customs, it was hard work. But I like a challenge, so I decided to give it a go. But I didn't really know how it was going to pan out." Babs

And then, one day in August 2008

"We took a very big coach and we went to Heathrow and then went all the way to Japan. I don't think any of us realised how

enormous it was. We wanted to go, we wanted to meet the Japanese young people but we also wanted to see Japan and we wanted a little holiday. So it was definitely a bit of a shock learning how to work, 8am to 8pm some days. But it was fantastic." Geo

Everyone had jet lag, but went straight into a whirl of activity. A report of the visit describes how the group was

"greeted at the airport by a group of young people and NHK television who filmed our arrival. It was a very warm and exciting welcome and each member of the group was presented with fans and little flannels to help cope with the heat."

Later, there was a reception dinner at the British Council where "we all enjoyed a huge feast of food and talked to the many invited guests."

"Then we went straight to bed and we had to be up at 7.30 in the morning and doing a full day's work until 6, 7, 8pm continuously for a week and a half. Then we had about three or four days in Kyoto where we got to sightsee and just relax. And then we went back for the last bit." Geo

They rose to all the challenges, even though Frederick recalls feeling like the room was spinning for most of the first week!

"They were a fantastic group of young people. I'll always remember them, they were absolutely outstanding. They coped with the pressure, with the long days, the complicated programme. They spoke to groups, they gave peer workshops, they talked about their lives here as LGBT young people. They were stars, absolute stars." Babs

And they gave a lot back.

"Without those young people I don't think I would have survived it so I owe them a lot. I got a lot of support from them. We were in it together. They did their best. They put in 100% every day." Babs

And what did they get out of it?

"I think we all got a lot of confidence from exploring new places. Some of us hadn't been abroad before at all and so that was really, really good. And we gave presentations to the head of the school board in Japan, and we were part of a larger conference which was televised." Geo

The group heard about the differences and difficulties faced by LGBT young people in Japan. The report to Bristol City Council about the visit says that the
   "Main issues of concern arising from the conference for Japanese LGBT young people were:

- the very high suicide rates
- absence of LGBT information, especially in schools
- isolation and fear in the LGBT community
- extensive homophobia in schools"

Babs described how the Freedom members *"were able to meet with other young people who didn't have the same freedoms and privileges that we have in this country. It wasn't even mentioned in Japan. There were no laws or anything like that."* It was as if in Japan, LGBT issues were totally ignored.
   Because they were being filmed all the time, Freedom members had to find a balance between being

"really passionate about what we care about, and being silly. We had to grow up a lot while we were there, and learn to be a lot

more professional than we'd thought, which was really useful. We made these vast connections with people on the other side of the world and learned how they experience life as an LGBT person. We definitely got a lot out of it in that respect." Geo

Eight years on, the excitement and enthusiasm is still infectious.

Everyone came home with a lot of amazing memories

... including the language

It's hard to remember a complicated language years later, but Geo and Frederick still recall the "polite hellos, goodbyes, how are yous?" and the respect that is built into Japanese culture through its language, such as adding 'San' to the name of an older person as a sign of respect.

"To this day, the most important phrase in Japanese will continue to be, 'where do you keep the food?', which is 'nabe mono wa desu ka?' Because I was a very hungry teenager and I was very concerned that I needed to make sure there was food, and also to make a funny impression." Geo

... and the people

"The way the Japanese are so kind and so generous and so giving, I really liked that about Japan." Frederick

... and the culture

"It was just so clean! When I tell people I've been to Japan, and they ask me what it's like I say, 'it's clean, there's hardly any dirt

Freedom members meet the Japanese exchange young people after arriving in Japan

anywhere.' It's almost immaculate. Frederick

The group visited shrines and temples, and saw the Buddha of Nara (the Big Buddha, one of the largest carved Buddhas in the world) which was beautiful and astonishing. They met with some Buddhist monks who told them about the religion and offerings made to Buddha.

"Oh, the Zen gardens, they're something else. In real life they make shapes in the stones or the gravel so you can't actually see the shape but, because you're in a relaxed state of mind, it's all about being calm and connected to the garden, you start to see shapes. I was a little bit taken aback, but it was fantastic." Frederick

... and the wildlife

The wildlife was memorable – monkeys, white deer, hornets.

> *"You remember the hornets? We saw hornets, Japanese hornets and they're – I probably can't describe them but they're big and they're horrible. There's warning signs everywhere saying beware hornets."* Frederick

Sadly, the *"exchange"* part of the project didn't happen. It became impossible for the Japanese group to raise the money for a planned visit by Japanese young people to Bristol. Freedom members were disappointed by that. *"It's definitely their turn"* (Geo). Maybe another year?

What Freedom did next Part 2: Back to The Voluntary Sector

In 2012, the Coalition Government instituted severe austerity policies. This meant that local authorities faced serious cuts to the money they received from the Westminster government. As a consequence, they were forced to make big cuts to their budgets.

• Bristol City Council cut its Youth Services budget by 40%
• North Somerset Council cut its Youth Services budget by 71% over 3 years
• South Gloucestershire Council reduced its youth services funding by 23%.

Bristol City Council commissioned outside organisations to run services and facilities for children and young people. Commissioning involved setting up contracts with other organisations and paying them to run the services that used to be provided by the Council. For Freedom members and other people using services, as long as services continue to exist, this isn't particularly relevant. But it has a big impact on the ability of organisations to provide local services.

In Bristol, all youth and play services became known as "Bristol Youth Links" which was described as "the umbrella brand that identifies the range of joined up youth and play services for children and young people aged 8-19." The Council developed a commissioning plan, and started to award contracts in September 2012. One of the contracts is for "specialist youth services" including services for LGBT young people. The other specialist services under this contract are drugs and alcohol, sexual health, emotional health, homelessness, relationships and sexuality.

This part of the contract was to be delivered by a consortium, or group, of agencies including Bristol Drugs Project, Off the Record, 1625 Independent People, Brook (initially), the Prince's Trust and the Family Centre for Deaf Children. Setting this group up wasn't a particularly easy process. Just as the bringing together of BYLBG and Freedom all those years earlier was a bit fraught, so was this. But in time, most of the consortium members thought that the specialist services contract created a pretty good mechanism for the sharing of information and ideas about young people's needs, and for dialogue between providers and commissioners.

OK, so this really is not all that interesting, but it is important in Freedom's story. At the start of the "Bristol Youth Links Specialist Services Contract", Freedom was managed by Brook. There were some bumps in the road and in 2014 the management was taken on by Off the Record Bristol (OTR), a charity which runs various services and projects with and for young people to promote and improve young people's mental health and wellbeing. OTR has had a long relationship with Freedom Youth. Babs was its Contracts Manager when she worked for Bristol City Council and was running Freedom Youth. From about 2006, it had been providing specialist counselling, funded in part through the money that Bristol City Council put towards LGBTQ+ services.

"It's been amazing to see it blossom again. It has burst back out after some difficult times, and become stronger. We've got more staff and more members. It's great to be a part of that." Thom

OTR remains committed to supporting and promoting Freedom Youth as part of its overall services. The future is never certain, but LGBTQ+ young people know that

"Freedom is here. It's on at this time and even if I can't go this week, it'll be there next week. Having that consistency is an absolute joy." Mitch.

Free to be me

The ten years since 2005 have seen huge changes in LGBTQ+ visibility, and there is legislation that supports all sorts of aspects of LGBTQ+ life. But young people who know or think they are outside 'the norm' face a difficult journey.

In 2005 the Criminal Justice Act gave the courts powers to give tougher sentences for homophobic crimes, and in 2008 "incitement to homophobic hatred" became a criminal offence. In 2007 it became illegal to discriminate against people because of their sexual orientation or gender identity when providing goods and services. Civil Partnerships, which had been legal since 2004, were permitted on religious premises in 2011. In 2013, the Marriage (Same-Sex Couples) Act was passed. LGBTQ+ couples could now get married just like any other couple.

And there are many more LGBTQ+ people in the public eye. There is greater acceptance and generally less outrage. In 2013 Alan Turing, the World War Two code-breaker who also played a vital role in the development of computers was given a posthumous royal pardon. In the 1950s, he had been convicted for 'homosexual activity' and took his own life as a consequence. In 2013, Olympic diver Tom Daley became one of the very few still-active sportsmen to come out. In

2014 the UK's biggest new musician of the year, Sam Smith, came out before releasing the debut album that propelled him to the top of the radio charts. "I kind of felt like I just had to mention it" he said. In the same year, the film 'Pride' was nominated for a Golden Globe for Best Motion Picture. In 2015, Caitlyn Jenner came out very publically as trans and in the UK Rebecca Root was cast as Judy in 'Boy Meets Girl' one of few trans actors in a mainstream television show.

And a story that was all over the media in April 2016 was the news that **Smithers officially came out as gay on 'The Simpsons."** #smitherscomingout. That this storyline had such a big reveal, and was reported across the mainstream media in the USA and Britain, just goes to show that being openly LGBTQ+ is still A Big Deal.

But having a different model of your life, one that involves knowing you are not heterosexual even if you don't know what you are instead… it's not easy. A lot of people think that someone's sexuality is public property – that they have the right to comment.

But it's still not easy, and we are still made to feel different. Freedom turns that on its head.

It just gave you that opportunity to be normal

Life is rarely normal for teenagers. And if you don't fit the culture around you, it's even more difficult. So, one of the gifts that young people most appreciate about Freedom is that it is a regular and reliable, and everyone feels ordinary and accepted.

"Well, a normal part of being a teenager is just having fun with people, you know, having relationships with people. Without Freedom, you would be more isolated." Max

"Freedom's brilliant because it was just a place where you could go and chat to other people and there was no other agenda. It was just a safe space." Paul

"A space that we knew that we could go to every week, that we could rely on. Even if we weren't doing anything, except for possibly making a sandwich in the kitchen, we could rely on Freedom to always be there. As a teenager, a lot of different things are changing. You're experiencing a lot of different things in school or at home and so having this base was really, really important." Geo

Freedom gives young people a base and a sense of security in a world which is too often hostile about different identities.

"They can go and be themselves for those two hours. It's a safe environment with like-minded people." Sue

There's a load of psychology and theory that says that if the basic stuff in life isn't right, if your basic needs aren't met and you don't feel safe and you feel that no-one cares, then it's really hard to grow into a strong and healthy adult.

"Freedom gave me a feeling of being settled, of a constant home. It gave me a confidence which I don't think I would have attained elsewhere. It was very good at bolstering you up, so you are OK to be who you are and to feel a lot of love for who you are. And to respect other people, and that's absolutely wonderful." Geo

"It gave me confidence, it made me happy, it made a massive difference. And knowing there's the support as well. When you do have issues, or you're down or the boyfriend's split up with you, sometimes just having someone to talk to, who can just have a quiet chat, it made a massive difference." Paul

This support too often doesn't come from any place else. Families can feel all at sea when their children come out to them. Friends may or may not be accepting. Workplaces may not want to know.

Freedom has helped young people to navigate their way through finding themselves and asserting their identities in the world beyond the Tuesday evening sessions. Starting with coming out.

Coming Out

"I wore a t-shirt that said 'I like girls in a Gay Way'. If that doesn't give the proper message, I don't think anything does." Rosa

But for many young people, it's not so straightforward. Many said that they found the confidence to come out through Freedom.

"I was so scared of coming out to my friends because I was scared that I was going to lose them. But when I went to Freedom, the amount of support and acceptance that I got, I knew that when I did tell my friends it wouldn't matter if they didn't want to know me because I had such an amazing group of friends at Freedom that I know would support me, no matter what. So it just gave me a massive boost of confidence, just to accept who I am and to let everyone else know, because I became comfortable with who I am." Tianna

"I'll always remember my first night at Freedom. I said it was something completely different to my parents, not an LGBT youth group. And then I came out of the first night feeling very empowered, and went straight home and came out to my parents, which they actually took rather well. Just having that confidence, meeting other like-minded people." Vicci

People choose to be out in different parts of their lives. Freedom gives young people the space to work this out and to feel supported in making decisions about who, where, when and how to come out. It gives young people a space where they can be themselves, even

Advice on coming out to parents

When Sue Allen was on Freedom's Management Committee, she was often around the building on a Tuesday evening. She had many conversations with young people about coming out to their parents. Sue has years of experience of supporting parents with LGBT children, and thinks that it's almost always better for them to know about their children's choices about gender and sexuality. Her advice is to

"Be brave. But choose your time carefully. Please don't do it on Christmas Day, when you're all sat round having lunch. Don't do it when your brother or your sister's getting married. Please don't do it on Mother's Day! Quite often a young person comes in from the pub, they're drunk, they knock on mum's bedroom door, go in and lie on the bed, and say 'I've got something to tell you". It's not the best time. And don't do it on the phone, don't do it as you're waving goodbye, when you're on the train. Don't yell out down the platform, 'oh and by the way I'm gay'.

I try and encourage young people to come out, and I say, 'go armed with all our information'. If they explode, they explode, don't take it personally. You've forced them to get out of their safe box that society puts them in.

And give parents time. They are not likely to 'oh that's brilliant, darling, I'm so thrilled for you, let's have a party'. Some do. But most have to process it. Remember how long it took before you told somebody you were gay from the time that you knew you were? You have to give your parents the same time."

Refer to the FFLAG Book – How do I tell my parents
www.fflag.org.uk/index.php/resources/downloads

if they are in the closet elsewhere in their lives.

"I wasn't very out in my jobs. I was out to a few people at work, but I felt quite lonely and different. It was very hetero-centric in my office so it was good to feel part of a gang or a close supportive community at Freedom." Rachel

"We had people coming who could not be out because they'd be in danger, so we had this very big sense of protectiveness around each other." Geo

"Some people may want to do a big coming out but you don't have to." (Rosa) In any case, you don't just do it once, even if large parts of your life are led in the public eye.

"Coming out is a journey, a never-ending process. I've been out for more than half my life and I've been a public person in Bristol for a long time, but there are still people who I meet who will ask me if I'm married and have children and of course they mean, am I married to a woman. I think most people still have to continuously out themselves." Stephen Williams (MP for Bristol West, 2005-2015)

It was easier for some people than for others to come out,

"So Freedom would run projects about coming out, the best way to come out. Kind of like the do's and don'ts." Frederick

And sometimes, none of this mattered. Sometimes, those Tuesday evenings at Freedom

"Just provided a safe space where we didn't actually have to talk about being LGBT and that was important in itself. Things were normal at Freedom which is very good for a teenager." Geo

Being me: finding myself

"Being part of Freedom allowed me to be myself. I didn't have to pretend to be anybody else anymore. I met lots of people like me. People who didn't fit into some neat and tidy stereotype of what it means to be female. I made lots of friends at Freedom – after leaving school early, I'd lost anyone that I might have called a friend. Being a member of Freedom gave me a lot of confidence and I began to assert myself when people weren't treating me right." Issy

The acceptance was for members, visitors and workers.

"The first time I went to Freedom was for my Youth and Community Work Placement. It was absolutely buzzing and I was really welcomed. I had a really lovely response from young people. You know, I probably looked a little bit like some crazy dyke at the time. I think I had a full Mohican and DMs and colourful clothes because that's the kind of visibility I liked." Mitch

"I remember a young lad whose mum would bring him, and he was in an all-boys' school and he'd arrive with various shades of nail varnish and lipstick on. It was his night. He could be as free as he felt he could and mum would support it – for that night he could be who he was. The joy in sharing that with him was fantastic." Adrian

Everyone, from the people who set Freedom up and the members in 1995 through to members today, say that this is one of the most important and highly prized qualities of Freedom Youth.

"It doesn't matter what kind of era it is; it can be stressful for anyone trying to find out who they are. It doesn't even have to be sexuality, just finding out who you are as a person is stressful

enough. Freedom needs to be there to help young people come to terms with things that they might not know or understand." Tianna

"When you're young and you don't know whether you're coming or going and you think am I gay? I don't know. I thought I was going to get married and have kids and everything was going to be normal. And then you go to Freedom you find out what you are. Then you think, I'm comfortable, this is where I am." Paul

That hasn't changed. The early members of staff remember that supporting young people to come to terms with their sexualities when Section 28 was in force was a tall order. But the need for support with your identity is as complicated and fraught today as it was in 1995.

"The outside world is becoming more accepting but I still feel that Freedom's the place you can be fully what you are. Lots of people still experience homophobia in the street and in their family. The outside world has not understood what they are or even tried to understand. In Freedom, we are all making more of a conscious effort. We know it's OK to ask questions, we listen, and we change what we think." Rosa

"A heterosexual guy can just openly say to his friends: 'she's hot', whereas this is just not something I could talk about in my world outside of Freedom. Freedom was a place where I met people who understood me and where I was accepted for going completely against the norm, a girl who didn't know how to be what society suggested a 'girl' was meant to be like. I started to see my 'difference' as cool and normal." Issy

The acceptance young people feel in Freedom is a crucial ingredient that adds to its value, success and longevity. People refer to Freedom as their 'family' because they feel accepted regardless of their personal identity.

"Why are we all labelling ourselves? It's a process you have to go through to find out who you are. Once you've found out you don't actually need that label." Paul

There has been a change throughout Freedom's life time, both within the group and beyond. Initially, Freedom Youth defined itself as an LGB group. By 2006, it was an LGBT group. In 2013, it became a group for all LGBTQ+ young people. This represents a wider social transformation which has seen Freedom addressing a diversity of identities, and supporting young people to be themselves. Whatever that self might be.

"When I first started the emphasis was on people being supported with their sexuality. One of the real changes that we've seen is the number of young people who are now exploring their gender within the group." Hannah

In 2016, trans and gender diverse people are more visible and are part of a wider dialogue than before. *"In the wider media there are more out trans celebrities…than there were even two years ago."* (Hannah) And so organisations working with young people

"… are becoming more inclusive. We've all got a gender, we've all got a sexuality. Different young people might have different needs, but equally they're all young people. We are seeing a beautiful family of identities and similarly with gender. We're exploring and experiencing gender in different ways and I think we need to view it more as a sexuality and gender movement now. And I think that by supporting a young person around their identity more broadly, we're going to actually deliver a better service for young people." Henry

Postcard produced as part of the Under Exposed Project 1998

This inclusivity is experienced within Freedom

"At Freedom you can define yourself however you want, as long as you're comfortable and happy with it. So many people want to make a big song and dance of identities. 'Oh this explains why you were so into dungarees when you were a child' or 'ah that explains that whole thing with that girl next door who you had some weird obsession with'. At Freedom you are just accepted."
Rosa

"What's phenomenal for me is seeing so many young people who are maybe exploring gender or sexuality and feeling supported with that. I try every single day to be the kind of adult that I wish I'd had at that age to have been able to talk about gender, talk about sexuality. For me, the most wonderful part is hearing so many young people's stories, both positive and negative, and then being able to support them to achieve what they'd like to do." Henry

Freedom continues to become ever more diverse.

"The range of identities has changed a lot. I remember that at my first session we had one trans man and one gender queer person. Now, at some sessions, there are fewer cis people than other identities. People have so many different gender expressions within the LGBTQ+ community. It's really cool that we've got such a diverse group now. Outside of Freedom, it's like society wants to be one thing or another. If you're not part of the binary, which can be the binary of man/woman or of being gay/straight, there's no other ground. But at Freedom, you can define yourself however you want as long as you're comfortable with it. And if you are not ready to define yourself, or if you want to try different identities, then that's fine too." Rosa

But it's still there, every Tuesday, running sessions, offering support and acceptance, celebrating young people's decision making, delivering friendship, community… and being a lot of fun.

> *"Everything else around the world changes but a lot of the things in Freedom stayed very much the same."* Geo

"Like lotus flowers unfolding"

Freedom may have stayed the same, but its members have always changed as they grow in confidence throughout their time in the group.

All of the people who have worked at Freedom described their pleasure and their pride at seeing young people become stronger and more confident.

> *"I am continually amazed with the awesomeness of the young people that come through the door and how inspiring they are."* Hannah

Mo said that her favourite memories of her three years working for Freedom were all about the people.

> *"Seeing young people becoming empowered, seeing them grow. Coming through that door, not having the networks, not having the confidence, and just watching them grow. Like a lotus flower unfolding because you could see them coming into their own; and then not needing us anymore."* Mo

> *"Seeing the transformation in some of those young people who have been coming for some time. When they first walk through the door they can be really shy, and not look you in the eye, not be confident in who they are. And then seeing them grow over*

Has Freedom changed you?

• opened and expanded my perceptions
• constantly challenges me
• made me a lot happier with myself
• helped me come out more to family and friends
• made me more accepting of other people
• it feels more normal to talk about sexuality issues
• boosted my confidence
• more happy
• makes me more comfortable within myself
• now I can promote a more positive image

Consultation with members 1998

time – I see that as a real success of Freedom." Scott

"Every time we have a young person who is ready to leave because they no longer feel they need the services it makes me very proud." Vicci

Henry described being interviewed by a group of young people

"who were so inspirational, so eloquent and so confident. I was so bowled over by how empowered the young people were to be given that role, to be given that leadership and voice." Henry

Laughing together

Goodness, this is sounding all very worthy and earnest! For many people, the acceptance they find in Freedom comes from sharing laughs, jokes and stories.

> *"We always had such a laugh there. These were some of the happiest times of my life."* Issy

Right from the start.

> *"The opening night was such fun, but then we carried on. At our first Christmas together as a group, there were a lot of young people who came back for the night, and they were confident and out and able, but liked joining us."* Adrian

It was built in to the fabric.

> *"One of the most important things for me was that it wasn't going to be a doom and gloom group. We worked hard to put so much fun and laughter into it. We had young people in the group with mental health issues or other experiences. People wanted to come to the group because they knew they would get support but also because Freedom Youth was the place to be. It was fun every week."* Babs

Members and workers always tried not to take heterosexism and homophobia too seriously, or to counter it by using the Tuesday night sessions as times to laugh together about it.

And the energy put in by the workers was repaid by members.

> *"One year, my birthday fell on a Tuesday. So I turned up at Freedom that night and I was told that I had to wait in the reception area. I thought they were doing a party, but the next minute a couple of the young people brought me into the room to the music of 'This is Your Life.' And there, in the middle of the room was this chair. They sat me on the chair and they presented me with a book of photographs of me with the young people for all of the*

Freedom members dressing up for Halloween 2015

activities that I'd run. One of the older volunteers had worked with the young people and the staff to put together an album, just like 'This is Your Life'. And then they went through all the pages, telling the stories. It was brilliant!" Babs

Freedom members and workers described some of their favourite moments in Freedom over its 21 years. They talked about the laughs and the jokes, the activities during regular sessions. They talked about making pancakes, playing games – Wink Murder & Forfeits were highlighted – and about creative writing or crafts sessions. Badge and banner making feature as high points. Not just because of the badges and banners in themselves, but because of the discussions that go into this and the way in which making badges allows young people to express so many different identities. And then, there are the trips that Freedom members and workers have gone on as a group.

When you meet a Lesbian: Hints for the heterosexual woman

- Do not run screaming from the room. This is rude!

- If you must back away, do so slowly and with discretion.

- Do not assume she is attracted to you.

- Do not assume she is not attracted to you.

- Do not assume you are not attracted to her.

- Do not expect her to be as excited about meeting a heterosexual as you may be about meeting a lesbian. (She was probably raised with them.)

- Do not immediately start talking about your boyfriend or husband in order to make it clear that you are straight. She probably already knows.

- Do not ask her how she got that way. Instead ask yourself how you got that way.

- Do not assume she is dying to talk about being a lesbian.

- Do not expect her to refrain from talking about being a lesbian.

- Do not assume that because she is a lesbian she wants to be treated like a man.

- Do not trivialise her experience by assuming it is a bedroom issue. She is a lesbian 24 hours a day.

From drama and role play activity 1998

"There have always been some interesting moments. The go-around at the beginning of a session always cracks me up completely. Today was hilarious, 'if there was a zombie apocalypse, how would you choose to defend yourself'. But mostly I just enjoy the normal Tuesday hanging out and chatting with young people, hearing about their weeks, them making me laugh, and just being in their company really." Hannah

Normality: whatever that is

For so many people though, favourite memories or happiest times at Freedom have always been "the normal sessions"

"When we didn't do much, when we'd just chill out, talk to each other and have this real feeling of comrades with everyone being happy with everyone else, everyone accepting. I'd feel that in here, I can be whoever I want, and no-one will judge anyone. I'd come away feeling that people cared, and have a warm feeling that it was a brilliant day." Rosa

Many Freedom members said they looked forward to Tuesday evenings because Freedom was the place they wanted to be.

"I just felt an overwhelming acceptance there. It was the main thing I looked forward to throughout the week going to Freedom, seeing everyone and just having an amazing time. It was great." Tianna

"I remember going on the first ever Tuesday and thinking, I just cannot wait to come back. Every week it was like, when's Tuesday, when's Tuesday, when's Tuesday? It's great. It's fun. And when you're under a certain age you can't go to pubs and clubs so you have to find someplace else to go to be with 'people like

me'. I just met some really good friends." Frederick

For workers,

> *"It was joyful to see young people looking happy, feeling like they had somewhere where they could share their story and express themselves. And where they could make real strong networks of friends."* Mitch

Because

> *"When you come through those doors it's like a big warm hug."* Vicci

7
Freedom today:
still needed in a still imperfect world

We asked everyone if they thought there was still a need for Freedom Youth today. Everyone said yes.

It's still not a perfect world.

> *"I would love to say, 'no we don't need Freedom', but we do. We have every bit of legislation but I still see a lot of homophobia, bullying, cisgenderism. I work in mainstream youth centres at the moment. I'm forever challenging homophobic remarks. It's not gone away, there's still work needed.* Babs

'The Teachers' Report' produced by Stonewall in 2014 describes a picture of still alarmingly high levels of homophobic bullying in schools: 86% of secondary school teachers surveyed say pupils in their schools are bullied, harassed or called names for "being, or being suspected of being lesbian, gay or bisexual." But more than half of schools now have a policy that explicitly addresses this, and 93% of secondary school teachers believe that school staff have a duty to prevent and respond to homophobic bullying. Despite this,

> *"There's still a lot of homophobia, particularly in schools. My working background was working in primary schools and in*

the playground, the word for anything rubbish is 'gay'. Yes, the homophobia is still there. When I talk to parents they often say that their children can sometimes face a lot of bullying in schools. And it's awful that some children are still frightened to tell their friends that they've got two mums or two dads." Sue

And while laws and social attitudes have changed, Stonewall's Homophobic Hate Crime Report, published in 2013, found that one in six lesbian, gay and bisexual people experienced a homophobic hate crime or incident over the last three years.

"Anyone who would like to say that things are fine now is in a deeply privileged position of not experiencing, seeing, hearing what's going on in the world. A lot of things haven't changed." Geo

For trans people, things can be even worse. Information produced by the Huffington Post in December 2015 reports high levels of mental health needs and alcohol dependency issues among trans people; 84% of trans people have thought about ending their lives, and a third have attempted suicide at least once. PACE, an LGBT mental health charity found that more than half of transgender young people had deliberately self-harmed. Most avoid some public situations out of fear. Evidence submitted by Equality and Human Rights Commission to the House of Commons Transgender Equality Inquiry in 2015 reports that 91% of trans boys and 66% of trans girls experience harassment or bullying at school, leading to depression, isolation and a desire to leave education as early as possible. The National Union of Students reported in 2016 that students who had experienced transphobic harassment in higher education were two to three times more likely to consider leaving their course. However, a major Canadian study, 'Being Safe, Being Me' reports that 'if someone had a supportive adult in the family, they were about four times less likely to have self-harmed in the past 12 months.'

Yes, there's still a need. And as young people change and identities become more fluid, there will probably always be a need. Kirstie Brewer wrote in the Guardian newspaper (February 2nd, 2016) that council youth service funding in England has been cut by 36% since 2011. There are now only 15 LGBT youth groups in the north-west of England, compared to 35 in 2010. All youth services are facing unprecedented pressures.

But current members say that Freedom still has a vital role to play as a place where

- *you don't have to hide who you are*
- *where I feel myself and can feel at home*
- *you feel a part of something*
- *I can make new friends*
- *you know you are not alone*

Most current members do now know other LGBTQ+ people, and coming out today is an easier and friendlier thing to do than it was when Freedom started. But the Tuesday evenings still give young people *"one night a week away from heterosexism."* (Babs) And Freedom current members assert that Freedom remains a rare place where *"we can just be ourselves."*

"We've come a long way with LGBTQ+ rights, especially in this country in the last couple of years. But the support that a group like Freedom can bring to a young person who is coming to terms with their own sexuality or gender, maybe they're not OK with it, or have no-one else they can identify with or talk with, no place else to get support…" Vicci

The bottom line is that everyone needs a place to find themselves, and to be with other young people who are exploring similar issues. Some of Freedom's earliest members reflected that

"I think it probably has got a bit easier for young people but not everyone's experience is the same. A lot of people still have grief with the family or from people at school. So you definitely still need a group like this." Max

"Recently, a young person said 'I'd really like to have a café for LGBTQ+ people that was serving cinnamon buns and coffee rather than the kind of alcohol and sex fuelled environments of the bars and clubs.' And someone replied saying 'that's called Starbucks.' We need both. We need the mainstream to be an OK space for LGBTQ+ young people to go and hang out in. But we also need the LGBTQ+ safe spaces because not all young people are confident and resilient and articulate enough to be able to get to the mainstream spaces and claim their identity in those spaces. Until society is so beyond labels, beyond identity, we're still going to need those spaces." Berkeley

Sue talked about the changing ways that parents are responding to their children coming out.

I don't get the calls now from the mums weeping hysterically down the phone. More often, it's mums ringing to say, my son or my daughter has come out and I'm looking for a youth group and need help. The age that they're coming out is a lot younger, mid-teens, which is why the parents are looking for youth groups. I google where they live and I just give them the information about their local group, these groups are springing up all over the place. And I always say that my daughter went to Freedom Youth and didn't look back." Sue

A bigger family of identities

Increasingly, Freedom is becoming a safe space in which to explore gender and identity as well as sexuality. Where no-one is judged and everyone is accepted for who they are.

"It's becoming more inclusive, supporting young people around their identity and by doing that, we're going to deliver a better service that looks at the needs of trans and gender diversion people, which might differ from young people exploring their sexuality. But they're all young people." Henry

"It's really important that people come together around shared identities and celebrate who they are. And celebrate not being judged and not judging each other. That can form a strength between people that can help fight injustice and discrimination." Hannah

For young people,

"It's just really good knowing whatever happens in everyday life, Freedom is still there as a place to explore what to do about things, and explore who you are. Where people say if you feel like that fits you, that's cool." Rosa

These days, there are more ways to find Freedom. Young people hear about it from the internet, friends, schools, through other services at OTR or through other health or mental health services. The numbers prove the need. Everyone working with LGBTQ+ young people agrees with this. At Freedom, *"we had to get more bean bags"* to fit everyone in.

"That safe space is still needed. Somewhere where you can go, feel safe and not worry about the motives that the other people have got that you're meeting. Straight youth clubs are just not the same." Paul

Mainstream youth clubs are much more open than they used to be, and more challenging of homophobia. But they are not the same. In Freedom, young people who would be in a minority anywhere else become the majority.

"You're born into a heterosexual environment. Freedom Youth gives a pathway to life, it gives you a support group. Freedom Youth is even more important now than it ever has been." Leighton

In mainstream youth clubs, young people

"are still hearing homophobia, they're still hearing transphobia. It doesn't stop, and it doesn't get challenged on every single occasion. So LGBTQ+ young people have to develop great resilience to a constant barrage of this language, because it's not always challenged by the role models." Mitch

It's not as though homophobia is a thing of the past; and transphobia is very much a thing of the present. In April 2016, the UK Government warned LGBT travellers to be careful in some states of the USA saying "the US is an extremely diverse society and attitudes towards LGBT people differ hugely across the country. LGBT travellers may be affected by legislation passed recently in the states of North Carolina and Mississippi. Before travelling please read our general travel advice for the LGBT community." OK, this might be in America, and the laws in question have been met with a wave of mainstream opposition. Even the Daily Mail reported on 25 April 2016 that "North Carolina legislators have already received a huge backlash from Hollywood heavyweights and officials across the country" and quoted the director of the Human Rights Campaign Global in America who "described the measures as 'terrible'."
In Britain, it's nowhere near as extreme. But in 2016

"I know that young people do have a lot more freedom outside

of Freedom. But there's still oppression." Rachel

And Freedom Youth goes beyond supporting young people to deal with oppression.

"It's so important for young people to have an experience of not being judged in the formative years of their lives. It means that you can later go on and feel a sort of pride in who you are. Freedom has given us a safe haven, and it's given us these opportunities that we wouldn't get anywhere else. Whether it's going to Japan or whether it's just making friends with someone who has a similar interest to you or being able to abseil down a 12-foot cliff. Whether you get to be part of a campaign or to walk in Bristol Pride. Or just feeling like you have a place where people are going to accept you." Geo

"We have been asked before, in a 100% perfect, everything's OK, everything's brilliant, nothing is a big deal, non-racist, non-homophobic, non-transphobic world, would we still need Freedom? And every single one of us said yes." Rosa

End Notes

he material in this book is drawn from interviews with past and present members of Freedom Youth, members of the original Management Committee and Freedom workers over the 21 years of its life. Choosing which of the many insightful quotes to use was a difficult task. We wish to apologise to everyone whose wise or wonderful words were left out. All of the quotes in **Free to be me** have been edited from the transcripts of these interviews.

We added to the interviews with an on-line survey of past members, and a survey carried out in one of the Freedom sessions in March 2016 with current members.

Current members further contributed to the book through an 'Opening Round' in April 2016, at which each person wrote 'What Freedom means to me'. All of the statements that were written that night have been included at the start of **Free to be me**.

Freedom Archive

We have gathered documents and other information about Freedom. This will add to the LGBT/Outstories Archive at Bristol Record Office and will be accessible to members of the public.

Particular thanks go to Adrian Murphy, for generously giving his Freedom Archive to this project and to the Bristol Record Office, and to Helen Webster for helping us to sort it out; to Berkeley Wilde for sharing his early records, and Beyond a Phase; to Ruth Jacobs for the calendar, postcards and posters; to Michelle McMorrow and Babs McPhail for their portfolios showing Freedom's early work and activities.

List of all interviewees

Some people asked us to use only their first names.

Freedom Members
Paul Stoodley 1995 to 1997
Leighton De Burca 1995 to 1999-2000
Max Thomas 1996 to 1998/9
Rachel 1997 to 2000
Scott Morris 1997 to 1998
Geo Leonard 2003 to 2009
Issy 2003 to 2005
Frederick Williams 2003 to 2011
Victoria Chalk 2007 to 2011
Thom Gray 2011 to 2012
Tianna Francombe 2010 to 2013
Rosa Fanti 2011 to present day

Workers, Freedom Youth Management Committee members – and others

Babs McPhail: Youth Worker, BYLBG and Freedom Youth; Bristol City Council Senior Youth and Community Worker for LGB young people; Freedom's Monitoring Officer; Freedom Youth Leader: 1993 (BYLBG) to 2012

Susan Moores: BYLBG member and Sessional Worker: 1991 to 1995; Youth Worker/Sessional Worker, Freedom Youth; Management Committee member: 1995 to 2000; Worker in Charge: 2000 to 2001

Julia Nibloe: BYLGB member and Sessional Worker: 1991 to 1995; Freedom Youth Management Committee: 1995 to c. 2000; Service Manager at Brook in Bristol: current

Helen Webster: BYLGB member and Freedom Management Committee member, Co-Chair and Treasurer (at different times): 1994 to 2000

Adrian Murphy: Youth Worker and Youth Services Manager; founder member of Freedom Youth; Management Committee member; sometime Sessional Worker: 1995 to 2006

Berkeley Wilde: Gay Men's Health Worker at Aled Richard Trust; Sessional Worker at Freedom Youth; Management Committee Member: 1994 to 2003

Mo Hand: Freedom Youth Development Worker: 1996 to 1999

Michelle McMorrow (Mitch): Youth and Community Work Placement at Freedom Youth: 1997; Sessional Worker; Admin Worker; Senior Youth Worker; Management Committee Member: 1997 to 2004.

Scott Morris: Sessional Worker: 1998 to present day

Sue Allen: Bristol Families and Friends of Lesbians and Gays (FFLAG): 1995 to present day; Freedom Youth Management Committee: c. 2000 to c. 2004

Victoria Chalk: Sessional Worker: 2011 to present day

Hannah Greenslade: Freedom Leader for Brook/Off the Record: 2013 to 2015

Henry Poultney: Trans Education Worker at Freedom Youth, working for Off the Record: 2015 to present day

Stephen Williams: Liberal Democrat MP for Bristol West: 2005 to 2015

If you want more information about LGBTQ+ history, here are a few places to look

- Outstories Bristol: For the social history and recollections of LGBT+ people living in or associated with Bristol, England www.outstoriesbristol.org.uk
- A timeline of lesbian, gay, bisexual and transgender history in the United Kingdom throughout the centuries www.lgbthistoryuk.org/wiki/Timeline_of_UK_LGBT_History
- Gay in the 80s website: www.gayinthe80s.com
- For the history of HIV in the 1990s: www.tht.org.uk/our-charity/Our-work/Our-history/1990s
- For information about Section 28: http://lgbthistorymonth.org.uk/wp-content/uploads/2014/05/1384014531S28Background.pdf
- For a summary of some important legal changes that have affected LGBT people in the UK www.youngstonewall.org.uk/lgbtq-info/legal-equality
- For information and research about trans issues: House of Commons Women and Equalities Committee: Transgender Equality: First Report of Session 2015–16, Published on January 14th 2016 (HC390) www.publications.parliament.uk/pa/cm201516/cmselect/cmwomeq/390/390.pdf
- Clare Summerskill, Gateway to Heaven: fifty years of lesbian and gay oral history, Tollington Press, London, 2012

General information:
- Stonewall: National campaigning organisation for LGBT rights: www.stonewall.org.uk Stonewall carries out research into LGBT issues www.stonewall.org.uk/our-work/stonewall-research
- LGBT Foundation: Manchester based umbrella organisation for LGBT people, with good resources and research http://lgbt.foundation/ LGBT Foundation also hosts the Evidence Exchange, "an evidence base of statistics about lesbian, gay, bisexual and trans (LGBT) needs and experiences"
- https://lgbt.foundation/evidence-exchange?page=2&search_input=Trans&topic_filter=a0HD0000009ewyvMAA&sub_topic_filter=0&min_year_filter=2014&max_year_filter=2016&filter=Search
- The Huffington Post often carries well researched articles about LGBT issues http://www.huffingtonpost.co.uk/
- Families and Friends of Lesbians and Gays (FFLAG) www.fflag.org.uk
- There is a lot more on line.